D1269562

A BELIEF THAT BEHAVES

A BELIEF THAT BEHAVES

An Expositional Study of the Epistle of JAMES

by

GUY H. KING

MARSHALL, MORGAN & SCOTT, LTD.
LONDON :: EDINBURGH

First edition - 1941
Second impression 1942

DEDICATION

THE REV. ARCHIBALD COCHRANE, M.A.

A quarter of a century ago, I was your curate at St. Matthias, Upper Tulse Hill. At that time you dropped a seed into my mind: you implanted within me a holy ambition to expound the Scriptures. That seed has long since grown into a perennial plant—a not very distinguished specimen; but, still, a plant of sorts. I thought you might be interested to receive some cuttings from the plant. Hence, I offer you this little book—an acknowledgment of my debt, and a token of my affection.

MADE AND PRINTED IN GREAT BRITAIN BY PURNELL AND SONS, LTD.
PAULTON (SOMERSET) AND LONDON

SOME WORDS OF EXPLANATION

About *the Title of this Book.* James was an eminently practical Christian, and he just could not conceive of a merely theoretical faith. I suspect that he would have listened with something like glee to the old Negro preacher who declared, "My bredren, dere be two sides to de Gospel; dere's de beliebing side, and dere's de behabing side"! You might almost think of this Epistle as an essay on that theme; or, if you prefer, as a sermon from the text of Psalm ci. 2—"I will behave myself". Yes, I think that A BELIEF THAT BEHAVES just about sums it all up.

. . . . .

About *the Nature of this Book.* For many years, one of the chief features in the life of the churches of which I have had charge has been the weekly Bible School. This ministry has given me great joy, and I believe it to be one of the most fruitful tasks that any pastor can undertake. I have been frequently urged to publish my studies. Well—here, at any rate, is one of them—a simple enough effort; but I pray that it may be found not unhelpful.

. . . . .

About *the Use of this Book.* I venture the suggestion that, before studying each section, the Scripture passage treated shall be read with close attention, say, half-a-dozen times. There are lines taken in the exposition whose point may be largely missed unless there is a previous close acquaintance with the text. Will you, therefore, do me the favour of using my book in this way?

Christ Church Vicarage,
Beckenham, Kent.

G. H. K.

CONTENTS

	PAGE
All in the Same Boat	9
God is a Great Giver	19
Seen in the Looking Glass	29
The Short-sighted Usher	39
The True Nature of Saving Faith . . .	49
A Subject that is in Everybody's Mouth .	59
Wise and Otherwise	69
A Few Home Truths	79
"D. V."	89
Money! Money! Money!	99
If the Outlook be Dark, Try the Uplook .	109
Camel-Knees	119

ALL IN THE SAME BOAT

JAMES I. 1-4; 9-15

1 James, a servant of God and of the Lord Jesus Christ, to the twelve tribes which are scattered abroad, greeting.

2 My brethren, count it all joy when ye fall into divers temptations;

3 Knowing *this,* that the trying of your faith worketh patience.

4 But let patience have *her* perfect work, that ye may be perfect and entire, wanting nothing.

. . . . .

9 Let the brother of low degree rejoice in that he is exalted:

10 But the rich, in that he is made low: because as the flower of the grass he shall pass away.

11 For the sun is no sooner risen with a burning heat, but it withereth the grass, and the flower thereof falleth, and the grace of the fashion of it perisheth: so also shall the rich man fade away in his ways.

12 Blessed *is* the man that endureth temptation: for when he is tried, he shall receive the crown of life, which the Lord hath promised to them that love him.

13 Let no man say when he is tempted, I am tempted of God: for God cannot be tempted with evil, neither tempteth he any man:

14 But every man is tempted, when he is drawn away of his own lust, and enticed.

15 Then when lust hath conceived, it bringeth forth sin: and sin, when it is finished, bringeth forth death.

ALL IN THE SAME BOAT

I. 1-4; 9-15

LIKE all Eastern letter-writers of the period, he opens his letter with his signature, and follows that with the address. Let us glance for a little at this paragraph.

"*James*"—who is he? Let us track him down. In Acts xv. 13, a "James" is presiding at the great Council at Jerusalem, met to decide the important question of the relationship of Christianity to the Law. In Acts xii. 17, Peter, released from prison, is telling the friends to go and tell the news of his safety to a certain "James"—evidently, again, a leader among the brethren. In Galatians i. 19, Paul is describing his movements when, following upon his three years' sojourn in Arabia after his conversion, he stayed just over a fortnight with Peter in Jerusalem, and met there another important church leader by the name of "James", said to be "the Lord's brother". In Acts i. 14, a number of people are recorded as meeting for prayer with the apostles, as they awaited Pentecost; and among them are included "Mary the mother of JESUS, and His brethren". In I Corinthians xv. 7, in the midst of the Resurrection appearances of the Master, we are told that "He was seen of James". In John vii. 5, is related the sad fact that "neither did His brethren believe in Him". In Matthew xiii. 55, we learn that the astonishment of the Nazareth townsfolk at the wisdom and works of JESUS was enhanced by the fact that He was but one of themselves, His mother and brethren being well-known in their community. One of these was a person called "James". Such, working backwards, is a sufficient outline of the career of the man who wrote this Epistle—a man who, from being a disbeliever, became an ardent follower of the Master, an important leader in the church, and eventually the president of the assembly. Let it be noted that, in the order of events, 1 Corinthians xv. 7 comes between John vii. 5 and Acts i. 14.

"*A servant of . . . the Lord JESUS CHRIST.*" For a score of years or more he had lived in the same home with JESUS at Nazareth. In that most intimate, and most stringent, of all atmospheres, he had grown up with Him, played with Him, worked alongside Him, daily observed Him. Who can doubt that He won the esteem and affection of His half-brother? Yet, when young manhood was reached, and JESUS went forth to His ministry, James, though amazed, could not bring himself to become a believer—with the others of the Family, he held aloof, and at times even conjectured that the One he had loved so dearly was now beside Himself. Long before ever James took up his pen to write, all this had been gloriously changed: the sceptic became the servant, the bond-slave; the half-brother was accepted, and acknowledged, as "the Lord". It is interesting to recall that a like metamorphosis occurred in the person of another member of that household: James' brother, Jude, also became a convert of the Lord, and also wrote a New Testament epistle, and also described himself, in his verse 1, as "a servant of JESUS CHRIST". Here is rich encouragement for any Christians who have in their homes members of their families who do not follow them in their allegiance to the Saviour. Keep on praying for them, and take fresh hope; seek grace from God to live in that home a crucified and risen life in CHRIST, and you shall yet win them to Him.

"*To the twelve tribes which are scattered abroad.*" I suppose that means in effect, that he is addressing this inspired communication to Christian Jews everywhere outside their own land. But, inasmuch as "they which are of faith . . . are the children of Abraham", Galatians iii. 7, all we believers have a personal interest in the Epistle's treasures: even though it does not refer to us, it does apply to us.

Even the most cursory reading of this letter shows that James is an intensely practically-minded Christian. Indeed, its main theme is not unjustly described as Practical Christianity. The writer is for ever relating truth to conduct, doctrine to life; and over and over again, as we study his manuscript, we shall find this emphasis upon plain every-day application. He loses no time in embarking on this course; he gets into his stride at once, and deals with—

A Common Experience of Us All

Trials and temptations! We are none of us excused, none of us immune; we are all in the same boat. Note in verse 2, and again in verse 12, the word "when" is used, rather than "if"—for the very reason that trial and temptation are bound to come, there is no "if" about it. These early Christians were subject, or liable, to all manner of tribulations; and, are not modern Christians beset with testing, though maybe after a different sort? Truly, then, this passage "speaks to our condition"—as is the habit of Holy Scripture.

Do you remember Paul's word, in 2 Timothy iii. 11, "What persecutions I endured: but out of them all the Lord delivered me"? I quote him at this point because of that "out of". He does not say "from", because God does not undertake to save us "from" trouble. Christian people must not expect to be spared suffering; but there is this lovely distinction—that, in our case, anything untoward can come into our lives only by God's express permission; it reaches us, not by luck or chance, but because it is His definite will for us; and if it is His will for us, it must be His best for us. Yet, GOD does undertake to save us "out of" trouble—either some miraculous deliverance of a material order, which shall glorify Him, or some spiritual release, which may glorify Him even more, as is instanced by GOD'S way of dealing with Paul's "thorn in the flesh", 2 Corinthians xii. 7-9. Another interesting occasion of this distinction between "from" and "out of" is found in Daniel iii. 17, "Our GOD . . . is able to deliver us from . . . and He will deliver us out of . . ." He could have saved them from being thrown into the furnace; He was perfectly well able to, of course, but that was not His plan, His will, for them. Those three young loyalists knew that they could not claim the "from"—though, in other circumstances, He might, and does, grant it; but they also knew that they could claim the "out of"—that, He is not only "able to", but "will" do. Out from the midst of your very trouble, your every trouble, you shall in some deep sense experience a GOD-honouring deliverance. "Out of them all"—says Paul. Whenever you find yourself in trial and tribulation, look out for His "out of"!

You will notice that trouble pays no respect to a man's social or financial standing. What has been said, and is to be said, will be found to be true alike for "the brother of low degree", verse 9, and for "the rich", verse 10. We are all in the same boat. But see here—

AN UNCOMMON WAY OF LOOKING AT IT

"Count it all joy," says verse 2. The words are reminiscent of something that the Master Himself uttered, in Matthew v. 11-12, "Blessed are ye, when men shall revile you, and persecute you, and shall say all manner of evil against you falsely, for My sake. Rejoice, and be exceeding glad. . . ." Often, when you look your trouble in the face, it is hard to recognise the blessing in it; but when you look back on it, you can see it all. Do you not think that the Sick of the Palsy thanked God for his affliction, whenever he dwelt upon it—reflecting that, in all probability, he would never have found the Saviour but for his grievous trouble? Many a sufferer has borne a like testimony. So, in faith and hope, let us learn to "count it all joy", until the time when our eyes are open to see it all, to understand it all. James is not offering us just a bit of easy-going philosophy: he is, by the Spirit, counselling us to a view-point which has deep reason behind it.

The poor man—note that he is a Christian, because he is termed a "brother"; but he is a stranger to comfort or luxury; bare necessities are not always to be come by; life seems to have treated him hardly. Well, so far as this world's estimates and standards are concerned, he is a person "of low degree"; but when he was "born again", he was born into a Royal Family. Dr. R. W. Dale said of him, "Let him remember that he is a prince, and glory in it. He is a prince on his way to his kingdom, travelling by rough roads, enduring many hardships, suffering from hunger, cold, and weariness, and the people among whom he is travelling do not know anything about his greatness; but *he* knows; let him glory in his high estate!" Thus may a humble believer count his very poverty his greatest joy.

The rich man—he is in a very different case if trial and tribulation come to him; he is so pathetically unused to the harder side of life. Bred, as he has been, in the lap of luxury, by the very reason of his riches, he has come to imagine that money is the Great Excellence of life. He is apt to judge life, and to measure his fellows, by the yard-stick of finance. Yet, in his capacity of rich man, he is really no more stable than the "grass"; the "burning heat" of some sudden calamity, of some unexpected movement of the money-market, reduces him to the mere ashes of his former self. Well, if this unlooked-for trouble brings him "low", so that he sees the perishable vanity of his "rich man . . . ways", verse 11, and so that he sets out to build another fortune, of the unwithering sort, that will make him, as Luke xii. 21 says, "rich toward GOD", then he will assuredly "count it all joy".

The average man—so long as he is one of the "brethren" of verse 2, may, then, expect to find fruit in his trial; for note (*a*) What it will do for us, what "perfect work" of character-forming it will accomplish. Sore trial may be most unpleasant for the moment—"nevertheless, afterward . . .", Hebrews xii. 11. You see, your hard circumstances are GOD'S tools—the Gardener's pruning-knife; "Supposing Him to be the Gardener", John xx. 15; the Refiner's purging-fire; "He shall sit as a Refiner . . . of silver", Malachi iii. 3; the Carpenter's cutting-edge; "Is not this the Carpenter?", Mark vi. 3. Such is the blessed function of tribulation. Moreover, note (*b*) What it will bring to us, a veritable "crown of life", verse 12, a deeply satisfying compensation for anything that may have been "endured". We must not forget, however, that these results accrue only to those who take the troubles aright—they will probably bring to us no good, if we are rebellious; but none can measure the good we shall gain if we take these experiences as from GOD'S hand, and let Him see that we trust Him, even if we cannot understand His reasons, or trace His purposes.

"*If any of you lack wisdom*"—to understand these things, He may ask GOD to enlighten him. We propose to study this paragraph, verses 5-8, later on, in connection with the teaching of this Epistle on the subject of Prayer; and we only stay at this point to express the view that the reason for the presence of this section here is as we have just indicated. We shall proceed to a closing thought about our trial—

A Not Uncommon Effect Of It

The testing may become a tempting: (*a*) *The Occasion of a Temptation.* Verses 9-15 appear to lead us on to this aspect of the matter. In this event, the believer must realise that the temptation is not God's responsibility. "God cannot be tempted . . ."—the place of temptation is foreign to His very Nature; "neither tempteth He any man." The A.V. of Genesis xxii. 1, that "God did tempt Abraham" is unfortunate; for the word should have been "test"—or "prove" as R.V. has it. Dr. Griffith Thomas draws the seemingly valid distinction, that—"Satan tempts to bring out the bad; God tests to bring out the good". Very well then: don't blame God if your trials become temptations to you. The Lord never intends that for a moment. The blame lies with your own heart.

This is seen in the explanation given here of: (*b*) *The Nature of a Temptation.* We shall none of us be disposed to quarrel with the words of verse 14, that "every man is tempted", in some way or other. Let us beware of becoming harsh, or censorious, towards anyone who yields to things that are no temptation to us! This experience "common to man", as 1 Corinthians x. 13 describes it, needs understanding. Our passage gives us what we might call the Mechanics of the Matter. There are two Elements in a temptation, an outward, and an inward. (i) "Enticed", is the outside attack of the enemy; (ii) "His own lust", is the inside attraction of the evil root of sin. "Lust" has not the specialised significance that it mostly bears with us; it means simply the strong desire and longing of the heart towards any (generally evil) thing. In a temptation, the outward and inward work together—Lure and Lust are in collaboration. It is as the Something within the Steel leaps to the lure of the Something within the Magnet; or, as a Spy within the Castle gets into touch with the Enemy outside the Gates. Such a conjunction inevitably produces an evil result, it "bringeth forth sin". That is the way of it, as the HOLY SPIRIT, through James, here teaches us.

Trials and temptations: yes, we are all in the same boat. The "escape" that 1 Corinthians x. 13 speaks of, is not an Escape From the temptation, that we may be able to Dodge it; but an Escape To Him that we "may be able to Bear it". He has pledged His very faithfulness that He will never allow the trials and sufferings of life to be too heavy for us. A pair of little arms were one day stretched out while father piled up goods for his small son to carry to the other end of the shop. As the wee person still waited for more, an onlooker said, "You can't manage any more". To which the answer came, "Father knows how much I can carry". Substitute the Father for that father, and I think we may usefully close this study with that story.

GOD IS A GREAT GIVER

B

16 Do not err, my beloved brethren.

17 Every good gift and every perfect gift is from above, and cometh down from the Father of lights, with whom is no variableness, neither shadow of turning.

18 Of his own will begat he us with the word of truth, that we should be a kind of firstfruits of his creatures.

19 Wherefore, my beloved brethren, let every man be swift to hear, slow to speak, slow to wrath:

20 For the wrath of man worketh not the righteousness of God.

21 Wherefore lay apart all filthiness and superfluity of naughtiness, and receive with meekness the engrafted word, which is able to save your souls.

GOD IS A GREAT GIVER

I. 16-21

"*Do not err*"—make no mistake about it, be quite sure of it. We do not find it easy to decide whether this verse should be linked up with what precedes, or with what follows; but perhaps we may spare ourselves the trouble of a decision by linking it up with both. Anyhow, this is true, that we may be certain of GOD's mind, both concerning the Evil—of the previous verse, and the Good—of the succeeding one.

"*My beloved brethren*"—a phrase that can become so hackneyed, so formal, so meaningless, or that may be so real, so full of meaning. Who can doubt that to James these scattered Hebrew Christians to whom he writes, were brethren indeed, and beloved in all sincerity? It is a happy thing to be "among brethren"!

Well now, in the section of this Epistle which we were studying last time, we were considering the Prevailing Circumstances of the readers, circumstances that, in essence, were not so very different from our own, circumstances of trial and temptation. This time, we shall be occupied with the grand fact of the Overshadowing GOD—a GOD who is atop of all life's circumstances, and who is able to lift us there, too, so that we need never again be "under the circumstances". And this GOD is a giving GOD. There is a legend told of an ancient kingdom whose sovereign had just died, and whose ambassadors were sent to choose a successor as between two twin infants. They found the little fellows fast asleep, and, looking at them carefully, agreed that it was difficult to decide; until they happened to notice a curious little difference between them—as they lay, one infant had his tiny fists closed tight, the other slept with his little hands wide open. Instantly they made their selection of this latter; and, sure enough, the legend very properly concludes with the record that, as he grew up in his high station he came to be known as The King with the Open Hand! It is no legend, but sober fact, that we have not a close-fisted deity, but a God with an ever-open hand—He is a great Giver. (i) John iii. 16 ever reminds us that "God so loved . . . that He gave His only begotten Son"; and (ii) Romans viii. 32 enquires, in consequence, "how shall He not with Him also freely give us all things?" Let us look into some of those "all things," as indicated by our passage—which reveals Him as,

The Giver of Benefits

We have here (*a*) *A Statement of His Benefaction*—"every good gift and every perfect gift is from above, and cometh down. . . ." That is to say, everything that is good comes from Him; and nothing but what is good comes from Him. How wide and all-embracing is this statement. Truly, His gifts are simply showered down upon us; and right gladly will we obey the Psalmist's exhortation, "forget not all His benefits", Psalm ciii. 2. We will remember them even if we cannot count them.

Our attention is then invited to (*b*) *A Statement of His Being*—for His Being is the explanation of His benefaction. The familiar description has a beauty all its own. "*The Father of lights*" is, of course, an astronomical figure. You will notice, as you study this Epistle, that its author is a great hand at illustration. Here he calls the heavenly orbs to his assistance, in order to elucidate his point. He, the Maker and the Giver of those rolling spheres is the lavish Benefactor of all who dwell beneath their golden radiance. As there are many "lights" up there, so there is need of many lights down here—the light of "wisdom", for which (verse 5) we have already been encouraged to ask; the light of comfort, the light of healing, the light of guidance, the light of understanding, the light of good cheer, the very light of life. All such come from Him, "*with whom is no variableness*". With that Great Light up yonder there is unceasing alternation between sunrise and sunset; but with Him who, in John viii. 12, announced Himself as "the Light of the World", it is always, and unchangeably, noontide. He is ever the same—for all times; and, also, for all peoples. He does not vary as between rich and poor, young and old, gifted and simple. He shows no change, "*neither shadow of turning*"—shadow caused by turning. Any shadow that comes between us and Him is not of His making, but of ours. An eclipse of the sun is no fault or failure of the sun; that darkening shadow is the earth's doing. So do we creatures of earth often cause a shadow to intervene between our souls and God. The only shadow that God Himself could throw is something very different, something wholly and beautifully beneficent. Francis Thompson has the idea of it, in his truly amazing autobiographical poem, *The Hound of Heaven*—

> "Is my gloom, after all,
> Shade of His hand, outstretched caressingly?"

Dr. David Smith, in his *Disciple's Commentary,* has a suggestive comment on the passage we have been working on: He says, "Grace is like the lights which God has set in the firmament to give light upon the earth; it is a sun which never sets. Where it shines, it is always high noontide, neither waxing nor waning; and where it rests, there is no shadow on the dial".

What boons the Sun imparts to needy Earth, and needy Man; and what benefits—far manier, far greater, far deeper—does the Father of lights bestow upon our souls. "Do not err, my beloved brethren"—make no mistake about it, God is a great Giver. He is—

THE GIVER OF BIRTH

That is true of (*a*) The natural birth—the truest account of it is that it is God's gift. I do so love to see, in the newspaper announcements of a new arrival, the simple words, "The gift of a son", or "of a daughter". It seems to me to be such a happy way of telling the world. But, of course, it is (*b*) the new birth—that is here in verse 18 to be dealt with. It is for James' friends—

Something that has actually happened, (*a*) *The accomplished fact*—"begat He us". (i) All need it—not only the bad, but equally the good. Even so good a man as Nicodemus needed it; for it was actually to him that the Master said, in John iii. 7, "Ye must be born again"! Of course, it greatly surprised him; but, then, spiritual life, Christian life, heavenly life, eternal life—call it what you will—is not something that, compared with ordinary life, is different in degree, but altogether different in kind. If a fish desired to become a man, and tried its very hardest to be better, it would only succeed in making itself a better fish: it would still fail of manhood. There is only one way, "Except a fish be born again it cannot enter into the kingdom of man". If a man desire to become a Christian, he will not accomplish it by being a better man; he must be different—"a new creature", 2 Corinthians v. 17. A man who is not a Christian, however good he may be, would feel quite out of place in heaven—well, like a fish out of water! Yes, indeed, we all need this New Birth. To return to our passage, we note (ii) They had it—and it would only have come to them by the one way, even as to us: the way of John i. 12. We do not forget that (ii) He did it—they could not accomplish this for themselves, however hard they tried. If ever we are to be saved at all, born again at all, it must be, can only be, His doing, as we shall now see.

Note in this verse of the New Birth (*b*) *The sufficient cause*—"of His own will". Not our merits or deserts, not our rights or efforts, but His Sovereign Will, is the sole originating, and effecting, cause—"not of yourselves", as we learn from Ephesians ii. 4-10, "but GOD". We should never have been regenerated unless He had willed it so. What we (somewhat loosely) call "conversion"—though we mean "regeneration"—is a matter of Will. You may work upon a man's emotions—and, within limits, it is not wrong to do so; for almost always it is Emotion that leads to Motion. You may get him to hold up his hand, or come out to the front, or use some prayer; but all is valueless, unless you have got his Will. It is a matter of Will—indeed, of two Wills: first, and foremost, and fundamentally, GOD'S Will, and then our Will. GOD says, "I will if you will". In our Marriage Service that is the essential feature. In answer to the challenging question, the man says "I will"; and, when the woman adds her "I will" to his, the wedding is an accomplished fact. So is it with our regenerating union with CHRIST, as part of His bride—our own "I will" is essential; but, even so, it would have been useless if GOD had not long, long, ago said "I will". Oh, wondrous grace!

And now for (*c*) *The mighty instrument*—"with the Word of truth". Whenever you listen to a believer giving his testimony as to the way in which he found the Saviour, you will find that sooner or later he will mention a Text which led him to the LORD. Perhaps it was John iii. 16, or Revelation iii. 20, or Acts xvi. 31, or John v. 24, or (as in my own case) Galatians vi. 7, or some other—but always there was a "Word of truth". Man's word was helpful to the seeking soul, but it was GOD'S word that really did the work. That suggests to Christian workers this rule:

in all your personal work, always lead the soul to a "Word", and leave the soul resting on that "Word". You will never make much of a soul-winner, unless you have learned how to use the Bible to that end.

One further truth is here in this marvellous New Birth verse, and that is (*d*) *The great purpose*—"that we should be a kind of firstfruits of His creatures". Perhaps that means that these early believers were the Beginning of the ingathering of precious souls, perhaps that they were to be an example of what all subsequent gleanings were to be, perhaps that they were to be an offering to the LORD after the manner of the old Hebrew feast. Probably this latter is the writer's allusion, for he is addressing scattered Hebrew Christians; and, in any case, it is certainly true that those who have been begotten of GOD, should yield their all to Him for His praise and His service. Old Matthew Henry says, "CHRIST is the firstfruits of Christians; and Christians are the firstfruits of creatures".

What a verse this is. Before passing on, let me say once more, "Do not err"—make no mistake about it, be quite sure about it, that you have received, in receiving CHRIST, GOD'S great gift of Birth. Nothing could be more important than this thing, upon which hangs your eternal welfare. Having settled that, we are now ready to consider Him in one further aspect of His giving love, to see Him as—

THE GIVER OF BREEDING

It is quite evidently His purpose that we should not only have Life, but that, also, that Life shall be of a fine quality—happily healthy, well-nourished, attractively influential, having all the marks of spiritual good-breeding: Heaven's gentlemen and gentlewomen. This is the theme that the HOLY SPIRIT now leads James to enlarge upon in the closing three verses of this section; and you will observe that Breeding is linked up with the Book. This James is a rare man for the Bible!

He teaches us that if the Scripture is to have this saving and sanctifying effect upon us, we must give it (*a*) *Careful attention*—(i) "Swift to hear": picture of the eager learner, ever listening for the SPIRIT'S voice in these inspired pages. Do we come thus longingly to our Bibles day by day—hurrying to hear, because we love the One who speaks, and because we know both the sweetness, and the importance, of what He says? How greatly He will reward such careful attention. Then, on the other side, (ii) "slow to speak": we have two ears to one mouth, that we may show ourselves twice as keen to learn as to teach. Yet we must not forget that we have one mouth—we are not to be silent Christians; we are, as occasion offers, to bear a testimony; "let the redeemed of the LORD say so," Psalm cvii. 2. The teaching then proceeds, (iii) "slow to wrath" —the learner becames the teacher; but the teacher must not become the angry partisan. Yet we note that "wrath" is not entirely eliminated—"the wrath of man worketh not the righteousness of GOD", but there is a godly anger, a righteous indignation. That Christian is gravely deficient in spiritual quality who has lost his capacity to be roused, and moved, and stirred, as his Master was—"ye that love the LORD, hate evil", Psalm xcvii. 10. Of course, we must beware of confusing temper with this noble trait: let us not hypocritically excuse and dignify our petty rage by calling it righteous indignation. Here is a pretty safe rule: if what has roused us is something that has been said, or done, against ourselves personally, we may be sure that our excitement is just sheer temper. "Wrath," then, has its proper place—but, "slow to wrath", even as He whom the prophet reveals as "slow to anger", in Jonah iv. 2. Be assured that these "slow" things will look after themselves if we give careful attention to the "swift" thing.

The fine quality of spiritual life that GOD wants us to exhibit also demands (*b*) *Due preparation*—just as a rich and beautiful harvest must be prepared for by a clearing of the field of all that is harmful and noxious. "Wherefore lay apart all filthiness and superfluity of naughtiness, and receive with meekness the engrafted word." Dr. Moffatt's rendering of these words is particularly vivid; he puts it, "Clear away all the foul rank growth and make a soil of modesty" for the word. The wickedness of our own hearts can so easily nullify the seed sown. Breeding requires Seeding; but there must first be Weeding.

And then must come, (*c*) *Actual reception*—the Seed given, which is the blessed Word of God, must be given a welcome to the heart. "Receive with meekness the engrafted [implanted] Word." Meekness is not weakness, as anyone may easily discover by trying to be meek! The essential meaning of it is—no self! Such an attitude towards the Word is bound to be immensely fruitful; and this Word, thus received, "is able to save your souls"—not from damnation, for he writes to those already thus delivered, but from damage, which they are ever in danger of suffering from those trials and temptations with which they were, and we are, surrounded, and of which he has spoken earlier.

We close our study of this section as we began it—by saying that GOD is a great Giver. The gifts of Ordinary life, the gift of Spiritual life, the gift for Beautiful life: all come from His hand, and His heart.

SEEN IN THE LOOKING GLASS

JAMES I. 22-27

22 But be ye doers of the word, and not hearers only, deceiving your own selves.

23 For if any be a hearer of the word, and not a doer, he is like unto a man beholding his natural face in a glass:

24 For he beholdeth himself, and goeth his way, and straightway forgetteth what manner of man he was.

25 But whoso looketh into the perfect law of liberty, and continueth *therein,* he being not a forgetful hearer, but a doer of the work, this man shall be blessed in his deed.

26 If any man among you seem to be religious, and bridleth not his tongue, but deceiveth his own heart, this man's religion *is* vain.

27 Pure religion and undefiled before God and the Father, is this, To visit the fatherless and widows in their affliction, *and* to keep himself unspotted from the world.

SEEN IN THE LOOKING GLASS

I. 22-27

JAMES is still talking about the Scripture. As we said last time, he was a great Bible man! Dr. Graham Scroggie—just such another—in his fascinating work, *Know Your Bible,* vouches for the fact that within the compass of this brief Epistle (5 chapters: 108 verses) there are references, or allusions, to Genesis, Exodus, Leviticus, Numbers, Deuteronomy, Joshua, 1 Kings, Psalms, Proverbs, Ecclesiastes, Isaiah, Jeremiah, Ezekiel, Daniel, and to seven out of the twelve Minor Prophets. That really is rather extraordinary. And, so far as the New Testament is concerned, the late Professor Mayor, one of the leading authorities on this Epistle, has said that he has found in James no less than 15 connections, not so much in word as in idea, with the Sermon on the Mount. A man, verily, steeped in Holy Scripture. Well now, I think we may glean from this paragraph that—

ONE OF THE OFFICES OF THE BIBLE IS TO ACT AS A GLASS

"Like unto a man beholding his natural face in a glass," says verse 23. That word "natural" is interesting: it means, "the face he was born with". You can't help your face, can you? Or, can you? Some of the ladies try, I am afraid, from the outside—I wish they wouldn't. If they only knew what "sights" they made of themselves! Let Christian women have nothing whatever to do with such things. But, there is a way—an altogether delightful way—of improving the face: from inside. The light of the Saviour's presence in the heart shining out in the very face—"they looked unto Him, and were radiant", as the American Revised Version translates Psalm xxxiv. 5. Yes, you can help the face you were born with by reflecting the Light you were new-born with. However, all this is an "aside". Let us return.

The mirrors of the ancients were, of course, not of glass, but of highly polished metal—mostly brass. It is strange to read that old time teachers used to recommend the use of these homely instruments as an aid to moral culture. Socrates, for instance, urged young men to carry and consult, a mirror—if they found themselves thus to be handsome, it would remind them that an ugly life was out of keeping with good looks; and if they were plain, they might remind themselves that handsome actions did much to counteract any impression of facial ugliness.

There are two ways of discovering what we are like—the photograph, and the looking-glass: the former so unreliable, sometimes flattering, sometimes doing scant justice to its subject; the latter so frankly dependable, and so unerringly truthful. The one is very like what people say of us—we shall rarely obtain a right estimate of ourselves that way; the other is what Scripture says of us—an infallible indicator of our real self. Take, for example, this corner of the mirror: Romans iii. 22-3—"There is no difference, for all have sinned". Here is a terrible jar for the one who thought he was so much superior to others; but this is the inescapable verdict of the looking-glass. All alike have the disease; some may have it worse than others, but all have it. Or, again, Jeremiah xvii. 9—"The heart is deceitful above all things, and desperately wicked: who can know it?" What a shock to one who has been brought up to think that the human heart is, at bottom, true and good. Yet, this is what the mirror reveals: it is no good arguing, or getting angry. Another instance of the mirroresque quality of the Word is to be seen in Romans

vii. 9—"For I was alive without the law once: but when the commandment came, sin revived, and I died." The meaning of that is not very clear, as it stands; but listen to old Matthew Henry's paraphrase, "I once considered myself alive, in the absence of the Law [the Scripture]: but when that commandment [the Scripture] was set up before my face, sin disclosed itself, and I realised my state of condemnation and death". Seen in the looking-glass, he turned out to be very different from what he had imagined!

Let it never be forgotten, however, that the Bible glass is not only intended to show us up, but also to clean us up. An interesting bit of familiar Typology will serve to make this clear. You will recall that piece of furniture in the old Tabernacle Court—the brazen laver. Its object was to provide cleansing for the priests ere they entered upon their further duties. Well now, how was that great brass washing bowl made? Exodus xxxviii. 8 tells us: "He made the laver of brass . . . of the looking-glasses of the women". What a token of the sacrificial spirit of those ladies! But how strikingly suggestive—the Glass, that which revealed the Need of Cleansing; leading to the Laver, that which provided the Fountains of Cleansing. So is the Bible Mirror meant to call our attention to the Amissness of Life, and then to point the way to the Amendment of Life; which is, I suppose, the meaning of that word in Psalm cxix. 9—"Wherewithal shall a young man cleanse his way? By taking heed thereto according to Thy Word". This, then, is amongst the blessed functions of the Scriptures. But, another truth is here—

One of the Dangers of the Bible Reader is to be Content with a Casual Glance

"He beholdeth himself," says verse 24; and the Greek word translated "beholdeth", the same as is rendered "beholding" in the previous verse, really means just "a casual glance". He looks in his glass; but so little is the impression made on him by what he sees of himself that he "straightway forgetteth what manner of man he was". I wonder if it has ever happened to you that, having looked at your watch and put it back in your pocket, someone has asked for the time, and you have had to pull your watch out again before you could answer him? Your first consultation had been so casual a glance that it made little conscious impression on your mind. In that same off-hand way do we sometimes look at ourselves in the glass; and such, say these verses 23-4, is the case of the man who reads, or hears, the Word and does nothing about it. His inaction is evidence of his inattention.

We ask (*a*) *What good will it do him?* He has dutifully rushed through his portion for the day, and has thus entitled himself to tick off the verses as read; but it has all been to such little purpose, that the passage has really said nothing to him, and certainly he has seen nothing of himself there. He has not been serious enough to notice the spots and blots that disfigure his spiritual countenance; and, consequently, he will "do" nothing about them—there will be no Cleansing, and no Correcting. Even if there was some momentary gleam of what spotted "manner of man he was", he was so little disturbed by the sight, that he has forgotten all about it as soon as the Book is closed. We say (*b*) *What harm it will do him!* Better almost not to have been a "Hearer", if he is not going to be a "Doer". In any case, this habit of inattention will grow on him, until he will find his reading simply and solely mechanical. "If any man will do . . . he shall know . . ." says John vii. 17—failing to do, he shall cease to know.

An illustration of this negative reading is appended, in verse 26. A man goes to the Mirror, expecting to see a thoroughly religious man; for he seems to be—that is, thinks himself to be—religious. What is his surprise to find that he is not the perfect being that he had fondly supposed. He has a glaring fault. One such is sufficient to spoil the whole picture—as James will subsequently teach (in ii. 10), "whosoever shall keep the whole law and yet offend in one point, he is guilty of all". The other day, a piece of shrapnel came hurtling through the window of one of my bedrooms, and through the mirror of the dressing-table: it is only one corner that is smashed, but the whole glass is spoilt! Our man's one blot, then, is shown up, his tongue is gravely at fault. James will show later in the Epistle how serious a thing this is. For the moment, let it be sadly noted that he does nothing about it—he "bridleth not his tongue".

Of this "hearer only", who is no "doer", it is recorded that he deceives himself, and disappoints his God. "This man's religion is vain." That does not mean that his regeneration is in question. He is still a Christian; but his practice, his "religion", is at fault—it carries no weight with God. Let us turn to a brighter thought—

One of the Purposes of the Bible Reading is to Induce a Careful Gaze

"Whoso looketh into the perfect law," says verse 25; and the word in the original for "looketh", signifies a careful, earnest, gaze. This man is so different from the other. He is an (*a*) *Observant reader*—giving good heed to what he finds. The Book is called a law of "liberty", because to "do" what it says is the secret of all true freedom—setting us free, not only from the defilement and disfigurement of those spots and blots that we spoke of just now as being revealed by the Looking Glass, but also liberating us from the very disease of which they are but the symptoms. This earnestly observant attitude to the word is no mere "flash in the pan", it is the habitual custom of this man's life, every day he bends his earnest gaze to the revealing page, it is his regular rule, he "continueth therein". Indeed, so earnest is he about it that we find he is an (*b*) *Obedient reader*—he is "a doer of the work". Whatever portion of GOD'S Book we read, we are sure to find something that it requires us to do; and, if we are wise, we shall at once seek His grace to be obedient. I say "wise", because, concerning one who follows such counsel, it is written, "this man shall be blessed in his doing" (margin). How vividly we are here reminded of the Story of the Two Houses, with which our LORD concluded His great Sermon on the Mount, in Matthew vii. 24f. How blessedly secure is the life there pictured that rests upon the Doing of those Sayings of His—not the Hearing, though that were blessed, too; but the Doing is thrice-blessed. "Hearers only" stand little chance in the inevitable storms of life; but the "doer of the work" finds himself empowered to meet all that life's vicissitudes may bring him, as well as equipped to use all the opportunities that may arise. Oh, to be of this quality of Bible reader—both earnestly Observant, and eagerly Obedient.

An illustration of this positive reading is given, in verse 27. The man goes to the Mirror to see a reflection of True Religion, and there he finds it. James, as we have seen already, is an intensely practically-minded Christian; he reduces everything to the terms of practical daily life. The HOLY SPIRIT, in using him as His vehicle of inspired instruction, does not abrogate that personality and mentality of his—when He speaks through James it is ever the practical side of things that receives emphasis. "*Pure religion and undefiled*", we may be sure, therefore, will be shown to be something so very much more than the merely theoretical, the simply mystical; "*before God and the Father*"—that is to say, "in GOD'S eyes"—it is, indeed, something most realistically practical.

Remember, please, that we are here dealing, not with Regeneration, but with Religion—its practical issue. James would have us grasp the fact that this latter consists, not in What we Believe, but in How we Behave. He is not the man to discredit Doctrine; none of the Bible writers do that. The importance of orthodox belief is recognised throughout the Scriptures as being fundamental and essential. The body cannot do without its skeleton of bones—"sound doctrine", to use the Scriptural phrase, is the skeleton of the body-spiritual: you cannot dispense with the skeleton, but it is desirable to have something else besides skeleton. A mere "skin-and-bones" religion is not the true New Testament type; and it is that "something else" that our writer is here underlining. James is evidently not altogether unacquainted with that kind of Christian who is the bane of our modern church life—the man who is thoroughly "sound", and thoroughly unpleasant! Not by the greatest stretch of imagination, or charity, can it be claimed that they "adorn the doctrine of GOD our Saviour in all things", as Paul urges in Titus ii. 10.

So, as in a Looking Glass, we mark the attractive lineaments of this GOD-recognised religion. Two sides of it are represented. The one is (*a*) Practical love—"*to visit the fatherless and widows in their affliction*". To visit, as contemplated by James, is not just to pop in and pay a cheery call. Perhaps the best way of understanding what is implied will be to look at another passage where the same word, both in the English and in the Greek, is employed. Listen, then, to Luke i. 68 and 78, "Blessed be the LORD GOD of Israel; for He hath visited and redeemed His people . . . the Dayspring from on high hath visited us". If we can take hold of some of the implications of His visit in those verses, and place them in the context of the verse that we are studying, we shall obtain a new, a higher, a deeper, a grander, conception of what is expected of those who seek His grace to be "doers" of this Word, "and not hearers only". Anyhow, no one can say that, in this aspect of it, proper religion is not practical!

The other aspect of the sort of religion that GOD wants of us is (*b*) Practical holiness—"*to keep himself unspotted from the world*". What a muddy place the world is! But, are we not told that it is GOD who keeps us safe and clean? Yes. In John xvii. 15, the Master prays, "not that Thou shouldest take them out of the world, but that Thou shouldest keep them from the evil"; and yet we are also told, in 1 Timothy v. 22, "Keep thyself pure". On some day when there seems to be nothing but mud and slush in the place where you live, remember that your Local Council has made provision for you to be kept unspotted by giving you a pavement to walk on, but you must also keep yourself unspotted by avoiding the edge of the kerb. So, avoid the kerb, don't run into temptation, "make not provision for the flesh", as Romans xiii. 14 has it, keep close to JESUS, thus keep yourselves, and GOD will see to the rest of the keeping.

So the chapter ends with giving us the impression of a man who has bestowed such careful gaze upon what he has seen in his Mirror that he has become a "doer of the work", and has enjoyed the "blessing" promised to all such.

THE SHORT-SIGHTED USHER

JAMES II. 1-13

1 My brethren, have not the faith of our Lord Jesus Christ, *the Lord* of glory, with respect of persons.

2 For if there come unto your assembly a man with a gold ring, in goodly apparel, and there come in also a poor man in vile raiment;

3 And ye have respect to him that weareth the gay clothing, and say unto him, Sit thou here in a good place; and say to the poor, Stand thou there, or sit here under my footstool:

4 Are ye not then partial in yourselves and are become judges of evil thoughts?

5 Hearken, my beloved brethren, Hath not God chosen the poor of this world rich in faith, and heirs of the kingdom which he hath promised to them that love him?

6 But ye have despised the poor. Do not rich men oppress you, and draw you before the judgment seats?

7 Do not they blaspheme that worthy name by the which ye are called?

8 If ye fulfil the royal law, according to the scripture, Thou shalt love thy neighbour as thyself, ye do well:

9 But if ye have respect to persons, ye commit sin, and are convinced of the law as transgressors.

10 For whosoever shall keep the whole law and yet offend in one *point,* he is guilty of all.

11 For he that said, Do not commit adultery, said also, Do not kill. Now if thou commit no adultery, yet if thou kill, thou art become a transgressor of the law.

12 So speak ye, and so do, as they that shall be judged by the law of liberty.

13 For he shall have judgment without mercy, that hath shewed no mercy; and mercy rejoiceth against judgment.

THE SHORT-SIGHTED USHER

II. 1-13

THE "brethren" belong to a glorious brotherhood. They are a company of men and women who are united in a bond of union; they are the number of all those who have "the faith of [that is, 'on'] our Lord JESUS CHRIST". This same phrase, bearing, I think, the same meaning of "on" for "of", is found in Galatians ii. 20. There are certain things that are wholly incompatible with such a "faith"; and one of those things is "respect of persons"—it simply will not mix; it is quite definitely unchristian. It is, alas, a quite common feature of modern Church life; but one is somewhat surprised to find its corrupting presence among these early "brethren". However, ancient or modern, the thing is wrong; and the always practical Christian who wrote this Letter proceeds to show it up, and hopes to cast it out. It seems as if some specific trouble had recently arisen on account of the behaviour of the usher, or verger, of some assembly—what a Help, or what a Hindrance, this official may be in a church community!

The particular "assembly" here concerned was, as the margin of your Bible probably tells you, a Synagogue. In such places, the senior authority was vested in "the ruler of the synagogue"—a personage so often met with in the pages of the New Testament; the inferior functions were discharged by one who was called "the minister": you will remember that it was to such a man that our LORD gave back the roll of Isaiah, after He had read the passage in the Nazareth synagogue, in Luke iv. 20. This official was a most useful person, and performed many duties—among which was that of seeing that the congregation was properly seated. It was in this latter connection that the particular one mentioned in our passage showed how short-sighted he was.

He Couldn't See Beyond the Superficial

On one occasion of worship two men came in, wanting seats. There was a considerable difference, even a disparity, between them. The one was clothed in "goodly apparel"—fur coats had not been invented by then; but you can picture the outward appearance of this man. The other was wearing "vile raiment"—but you must not go wrong over that word "vile"; it is used again, in Philippians iii. 21, of our "vile body"; it merely means, humble, lowly. So that this second person who caught the usher's eye that day was—poorly dressed, a bit ragged, if you like, but nothing worse. It was easy to see which was the better man of the two! Yet, wait a bit, Mr. Usher, are you quite sure that you are right in your estimation? Are you not a bit short-sighted? Is your judgment not superficial?

A man may wear goodly apparel—and yet his soul may be garmented in "filthy rags", as Isaiah lxiv. 6 says. This may not be so; but there is always the possibility. The point is that we must not judge by the outside of a man. There is an old saying that "Clothes make the man"; but I prefer the Winchester motto, "Manners makyth man".

A man may wear humble clothes—and yet be the happy possessor of a most attractive wardrobe for the soul. "*The robe of righteousness*", that Isaiah lxi. 10 speaks of, may be his; "*the garment of praise*", in the 3rd verse of the same chapter, may have been given him by his Lord—it is a lovely dress; "*be clothed with humility*", says 1 Peter v. 5, and that is a sartorial fashion greatly esteemed in the streets of Heaven; "*the whole armour of God*", so grandly described in Ephesians vi. 14-18, occupies a cupboard all to itself in his soul's dressing-room; and "*above all these things put on charity*", Colossians iii. 14 reminds us, and that is a glorious overcoat more warming to the heart than any fur coat is to the body. What a well-stocked wardrobe this is, to be sure; yet it may be possessed by a person who outwardly has perforce to wear very shabby clothes. I say "may be" because I am anxious, at this point, to guard against the idea that a poor man is necessarily good, and a rich man necessarily bad—the one may be as fine, or as evil, as the other. I repeat that the point is that we are not to judge anyone by outside appearance. To dispense favour on this ground, to show "respect of persons" on this basis, is not only utterly wrong, but uncommonly foolish—besides, it is so superficial. Well now, this usher's eyesight will again reveal its shortcomings by the test that—

He Couldn't See Beyond the Material

"A man with a gold ring . . . a poor man": why, there is no possible question, in our Usher's eyes, where his choice shall lie, which his preference shall enjoy, where his best seat shall be bestowed. Gold gets him every time: it is the highest he knows, for he cannot see farther than the material—the spiritual is beyond him.

The distinction made—is, anyhow, clean cut. (i) *The poor*—two words are used of him. He is, at one and the same time, both "chosen" and "despised". Which shall be our attitude towards him? Well, think a moment: it is God who is said to have "chosen" the poor. When it was planned, in the eternal counsels of the Triune Deity, that "the Lord of Glory", as our first verse calls the Saviour, should come to this earth and take human flesh, it was not to the stately home of the affluent that He went, not in the cushioned circumstances of the wealthy that He abode: a despised city, a humble home, a simple family—these were the circumscribed conditions of His dwelling among men. GOD chose the poor. When He went forth upon His three-years' ministry, it was the less highly favoured that He called around Him, and that were attracted to His side—there were some rich, but they were mostly poor. When He would illuminate the truth that He taught, it was to the lesser folks that He most often turned to enforce His lesson—to a Lazarus, in preference to a Dives; to "a certain poor widow" who had no more than a farthing to contribute to the collection. GOD chose the poor. And when He would recruit the army that was to carry His colours in the great campaign, it was from amongst the foolish, and the weak, and the base, and the despised, and the sheer nobodies that, for the most part, He filled the ranks, as 1 Corinthians i. 27-28 tells us. GOD chose the poor; and shall this short-sighted usher despise them? Shall we despise them? They are not GOD'S choice because they are poor; but they may be His choice although they are poor. (ii) *The rich*—on the other hand have not, as a class, done any service to these early Christians to warrant their preferential treatment. There are exceptions; but, as a class, all that they have done them is disservice. Dr. Moffatt hazards the suggestion that "James knew cases like those which occur in modern India, where rich Hindus will bully and persecute unjustly the poor pariahs who join the Christian church". On every conceivable pretext, their attitude is to persecute you, and prosecute you; and they do not scruple to pour lewd scorn on "that worthy Name by the which ye are called". It is said in 1 Peter iv. 16, "if any man suffer as [simply because he is] a Christian, let him not be ashamed"—the apostle did not say "afraid", because that was not the point of attack; but "ashamed", because it was the ribald ridicule of the world that their worthy name evoked. James' readers knew something of the jeering and sneering of CHRIST'S adversaries; and they were reminded that such things, more often than not, emanated from the supercilious rich. The "believers" of those days had little to thank them for—as a class—little cause to pay them court and honour. How purblind was this usher to do it!

The rule obtaining—was to be the same for each alike: both rich and poor were to be treated in accordance with the law of love. "The royal law", it is called; not because it is the first of laws—love to GOD occupied that premier position—but, as Deissmann seems to have established, in his *Light from the Ancient East*, because it was made by the King, the King of kings. "Thou shalt love thy neighbour as thyself"—it has, indeed, a royal air about it; and, if it is made the basis and guide of our thoughts, words, and actions, towards our fellows, "ye do well". Our relationship both to this rich man, and to this poor man, is to be governed by this portion of "the law of liberty". By all means, make a fuss of the rich, if, by the operation of "the royal law", it is going to help him; but, you mustn't do it at the expense of the poor man. If this latter be the case, then a just reckoning shall inevitably supervene.

The judgment coming—is plainly and solemnly underlined for our instruction and warning. Two things are said concerning this man's commission of the fault of "respect of persons", and this assembly's acquiescence in it. (i) "*Convicted*", in verse 9. This thing is said to be, not merely a breach of manners, but quite definitely a "sin"—and though a man were able to declare that he has kept "the whole law" with this solitary exception, yet he is by this convicted by "the law" as being "guilty of all": adultery, murder, "respect of persons"—it is all, and equally, sin. (ii) "*Judged*", in verse 12. The Christian needs to bear in mind that, as Romans xiv. 10 tells us, "we shall all stand before the judgment seat of CHRIST". True it is, blessedly true, that the believer has not to face the judgment of the Great White Throne, of which Revelation xx. 11 speaks—his eternal relationship with GOD, and his everlasting bliss in Heaven, are alike gloriously assured, in response to his "faith on our Lord JESUS CHRIST" mentioned in our first verse; but, for all that, he has a judgment upon his works, his behaviour, since he became a Christian—that judgment which is so vividly described in 1 Corinthians iii. 11-15, and whose severity is so plainly indicated by verse 13 of this passage that we are studying. Perhaps we had not realised that this habit of "respect of persons" was so serious—but it is always serious to break "the law of liberty", always serious to hurt "the poor", always serious to dishonour "the Lord of glory". I wonder if some of us Christians are rather inclined to a lax view of sin, seeing that, by the grace of GOD and through the blood of CHRIST, we have been saved from its penalty and eternal doom. I wonder if sin in a believer is not infinitely more culpable than in an unbeliever—even as an inkstain is far worse on a white dress than on a black one. I wonder if it is not one of the Christian's deepest needs to pray for a sensitive conscience. Well, it is one particular sin that is here under review, and the altogether false estimate of values that underlies it. See, then, further—

The wealth commanded—this is spiritual riches: open to the materially rich and poor alike. "The poor of this world", even that one whom you have perhaps been despising, may be enormously "rich in faith", and even an "heir of the kingdom". This wealth is not stored up in any earthly bank: these are "treasures in heaven" that Matthew vi. 20 speaks about. Good deeds, done in CHRIST'S name, earnest prayers, services rendered, souls won, days and powers spent for Him—these things, and others like them, pass for valuable currency in that place whose gates are of pearl, and whose streets are of gold. Of some rich man, the obituary notice will say that he left £60,000; while of some poor man, if he is a true believer, and faithful servant of his Lord, it may be asserted —not that he has left, but that he has got, a fortune that cannot be reckoned in terms of earth at all "laid up" for him in Heaven. How truly stupid it is to judge folks by their material possessions. Yet, this usher of ours was unfortunately so short-sighted that he could not see any further than the material; and I'll tell you another thing,

He Couldn't See Beyond the Temporal

I can see our splendid and worthy usher on the alert, about his duties, before the service began that day. I can recognise how quickly he sums up these two strangers, as they enter: he has a very clean-cut method of differentiating amongst people, as all "respecters of persons" have. He knows the respective value of each, beyond, as he thinks, any possibility of mistake. I'm afraid he is quite unaware of the defect in his eye-sight. Well, watch him as he puts them each in his place.

"*Sit thou here in a good place.*" We have said that this congregation was met in a synagogue, belonging to Christian Jews. If it were furnished and appointed in the usual way of such buildings, "the chief seats in the synagogue", which are referred to in Matthew xxiii. 6 as the places so eagerly coveted by the Scribes and Pharisees, would be that row of seats set with their backs to the Ark, where the scrolls of the Law were kept, and which faced towards the congregation, who would, of course, dutifully honour the distinguished personages who occupied such a conspicuous and exalted situation. This "good place" seems to the usher the most becoming seat for our expensively bedecked and beringed visitor. Whether, or not, he has any spiritual quality to justify his pre-eminence, the usher would not be concerned to know.

"*Stand thou there, or sit here under my footstool.*" He need not be offered any particular consideration. He is only a poor man; anything is good enough for him. If he doesn't care to stand during the whole service, he can sit on the floor. After all, he won't put much in the collection, so it doesn't matter if he never comes again. Perhaps we are doing the usher an injustice in attributing such thoughts to him—but, it's his own fault; he shouldn't have acted in such a way!

Well, he has put those two in their place. Yet, if he could only have looked beyond the temporal, and seen what were the eternal places of the men, he might have got both a surprise and a shock! Many a Humble person here will change places and become an Honoured person hereafter—"many that are first shall be last; and the last first", said the Saviour, in Mark x. 31. Simple, faithful, unthought of, souls, scattered about in, almost lost in, the congregation, how we envy you the place that He will assign you hereafter—and how stupid of us to have imagined that your present lowly place was anything other than just temporal.

THE TRUE NATURE OF SAVING FAITH

JAMES II. 14-26

14 What *doth it* profit, my brethren, though a man say he hath faith, and have not works? can faith save him?

15 If a brother or sister be naked, and destitute of daily food,

16 And one of you say unto them, Depart in peace, be *ye* warmed and filled; notwithstanding ye give them not those things which are needful to the body; what *doth it* profit?

17 Even so faith, if it hath not works, is dead, being alone.

18 Yea, a man may say, Thou hast faith, and I have works: shew me thy faith without thy works, and I will shew thee my faith by my works.

19 Thou believest that there is one God; thou doest well: the devils also believe, and tremble.

20 But wilt thou know, O vain man, that faith without works is dead?

21 Was not Abraham our father justified by works, when he had offered Isaac his son upon the altar?

22 Seest thou how faith wrought with his works, and by works was faith made perfect?

23 And the scripture was fulfilled which saith, Abraham believed God, and it was imputed unto him for righteousness: and he was called the Friend of God.

24 Ye see then how that by works a man is justified, and not by faith only.

25 Likewise also was not Rahab the harlot justified by works, when she had received the messengers, and had sent *them* out another way?

26 For as the body without the spirit is dead, so faith without works is dead also.

THE TRUE NATURE OF SAVING FAITH

II. 14-26

THE underlying object of this passage seems to be to lead us into a real understanding of what is saving faith. In the relation between GOD and man, there seem to be four different kinds of faith. The first is

A BELIEF OF HIM

Simply believing what He says. This is not discussed in our present passage, and I only mention it here for the sake of completeness. You will recall how that, in John iii, 12, the Master says to Nicodemus, "I have told you . . . and ye believe not". It is, alas, only too true that a large number of even Christian people disbelieve what He has told them—they would not worry as they do, they would not speak as they do, they would not reckon as they do, they would not behave as they do, if they really did believe what He says. This is a damaging indictment, isn't it? Yet, will you seriously challenge it? Some even go so far as to say that they find it difficult to believe—think of it: GOD has spoken, and they find it hard to believe what He has said. A man once went to Dr. Torrey and said "I can't believe"; and Dr. Torrey's blunt and unexpected answer was, "Whom can't you believe?" Not "what"—but "Whom"! A man should surely not find it impossible, or even difficult, to believe GOD. This belief of Him is the very least that He can expect of His creatures.

A BELIEF ABOUT HIM

"*Thou believest that there is one God*", says verse 19. James is addressing Christians who have been converted out of Judaism; and they will at once catch his allusion. He is referring to the great credal statement of Deuteronomy vi. 4f. —"Hear, O Israel: the Lord our God is one Lord: and thou shalt love the Lord thy God with all thine heart, and with all thy soul, and with all thy might". This was one of the passages of scripture that the Pharisees inscribed upon parchment and placed in the little leathern cases, called "phylacteries", Matthew xxiii. 5, which they bound upon their arm and their forehead, imagining that they must take the injunctions of verse 8 in a literal sense. All Jews placed, and place, a great deal of weight upon this confession of the "One God".

We know that there were many, and James evidently had some such in mind, who thought that if they had a correct belief, all was well, all was right. It is a dangerous mistake from which we ourselves are not altogether immune. We may recite our "I believe" in Church with all seriousness and sincerity, and yet it is possible that it is nothing more than a mere intellectual acceptance of historical facts—of no more moral value than the belief that Julius Cæsar came here in 55 B.C., or that William of Normandy began his conquest of Britain in A.D. 1066. Such belief about GOD, and what He has done for our redemption, has no saving quality whatever.

Nevertheless, let it be added that, as we said in a previous talk, James was not the man to discredit, or belittle, orthodoxy of belief. He knew its basic value, and would whole-heartedly applaud it wherever he found it, as he does here—"*thou doest well*". Only, he was anxious, desperately anxious, that his friends should not confuse that kind of head-belief, and the heart-belief, which is necessary to salvation. But, once more, we pass on to—

A Belief in Him

"*The devils also believe, and tremble*". It is a striking reflection that there are no atheists among the devils; they know too much to have ever succumbed to that delusion—they are, in the sense of our previous section, the most orthodox of beings. But, why "tremble"? Because these creatures believe, not only in GOD'S existence, but also in His power. They believe in Him, thus, because they are forced to do so. This is a stage further on in faith—but it is still not saving faith, as a little thought will reveal.

It may be that there is some doctor that you believe in—not because you have ever been to him for treatment, but because a friend of yours has. He handled that case so well, he secured such fine results, that you have developed a real belief in him. But something more would be necessary if he were to be able to save you from some malady. You know he can, for he saved your friend; but that, of itself, is not sufficient to save you. Or, it may be some patent medicine, guaranteed to be a certain cure for some specific thing. You believe about it—for you have read the glowing advertisements; you believe in it—because your neighbour got miraculous relief through it; yet, if you yourself are attacked by the complaint, your belief thus far is of no avail to you. Similarly, gripped as we are by the Disease of Sin, we may believe about Him who shed His precious blood for us to save us; we may believe in Him, that He is well able to save us as He promises; yet we have not come to saving faith until we take this last step of—

A BELIEF ON HIM

This is what James is concerned with in this paragraph. But, before getting to the theology of the matter, let me give you two simple little stories, which will serve to light up the nature of this saving kind of faith. (1) Blondin, the famous tight-rope walker, was upon one occasion waiting to commence his performance, when he noticed a schoolboy standing by, all agog with interest. Addressing him, and pointing up to the rope, he said, "Do you believe

I can walk across that rope?" "Yes, I do," was the reply. There followed another question, "Do you believe I could carry you on my back and walk across?" Unhesitatingly came the answer "Yes, certainly". "Very well, then," said Blondin, bending down, "jump up." But the boy disappeared. He had said that he believed, but——! (2) A grocer was down in the cellar of his shop, when he noticed his small son standing at the edge of the open trap-door. He called up, "Here I am, sonnie, jump down". But the boy hesitated. "I can't, daddie; I can't see you". Up came the answer, "No, but I can see you; trust me and jump, and I will catch you." Upon which, the step was taken—and, in very truth, he believed on his father. Bear those two stories in mind as we proceed.

You will not have failed to notice how frequently, when saving faith is spoken of, the preposition "on" follows the verb, e.g., Acts xvi. 31. If we are consistent in our translation, the frequency is more marked still, for in many cases where we find "in"—as, for example, in John iii. 14-16—the Greek preposition is that same one as for "on". In its turn, it governs the accusative case in the noun that follows it; and the grammarians tell us that, for this reason, it implies motion towards, or on to, the object. This makes of the belief in question a moving thing, a living thing. The three first kinds of faith that we have dealt with are all static; but belief on Him is the quality which takes us on to Him, to rest on Him—a movement of trust which Blondin's boy refused, but which the grocer's boy displayed.

A further little essay in Greek translation will emphasize, and underline, the truth we are expounding. If you will turn up again the familiar John iii. 16, you will observe the word "believe"—saving faith. If you now go to John ii. 24, you will notice the word "commit"— "JESUS did not commit Himself unto them". Those two are the same word in the original; and that seems to me to give us the striking suggestion that saving faith is, indeed, a "belief on", a committing of ourselves to Him, as the grocer's boy committed himself to his father. Any sort of faith that stops short of this "work" of committal is a "dead" thing—which can neither justify, nor save. This is the point that, as it seems to me, James is concerned to drive home to his hearers; this is the "work" that he sees to be an essential ingredient of saving faith—as he writes in verse 22, "faith wrought in his works, and by works was faith made perfect". Remember how, in John vi. 28, the people asked, "What shall we do, that we might work the works of God?" and how the Master answered, "This is the work of God, that ye believe on Him whom He hath sent". A belief on Him is very truly a working thing, a moving thing, a living thing.

Some have imagined that there is a quarrel between James and Paul on this fundamental matter. Martin Luther even went so far as to stigmatise our Letter as an "epistle of straw", because, as he thought, it contradicted Paul. Of course, Martin might be trusted to castigate anyone who dared to criticise his beloved Paul—especially in his beloved Galatians! As a matter of fact, the latest scholarship seems quite decided that James was writing earlier than either Galatians or Romans; in which case, any contradicting was done, not by James, but by Paul. But, in sober fact, was there any contradiction? Is not the simple explanation that they used the word "faith" in different senses? James says—"not by faith only", because the faith he is thinking of is that sort that we mentioned earlier: just a head-belief. No one would more fully agree with James on that than Paul himself. Paul says—"by faith only", because the faith he is thinking of is this last kind, the sort that works. James would enthusiastically agree. To this kind of faith, no other "works" are to be added, as security for salvation—as Ephesians ii. 8-9 makes abundantly plain; no other works, either ceremonial or moral, the work of faith only. Paul appeared before the council of Jerusalem on that very issue—the work of faith only; and the decision of that council, announced by its chairman, was entirely in favour of Paul's attitude. The chairman's name was James, Acts xv. 13—the very man who writes our Epistle. Nothing could more conclusively demonstrate their identity of view. The seeming difference arises, I am persuaded, from their differing use of the same word. But, enough of controversy: let us take a look at the personal instance of faith that James adduces.

First, there is Abraham—whom Paul also selects as his example, both in Romans iv. and in Galatians iii. We are taken back to the story, the wonderful and thrilling story, in Genesis xv. 6—where we read that "He believed in the LORD." GOD made him the magnificent promise that his seed should be as great in number as the multitude of the stars; and Abraham believed that. This was his faith; but, what sort of a faith was it? Was it of a "dead" kind, or did it work? The opportunity arose for putting it to the test, in Genesis xxii. GOD asked for the sacrifice of Isaac: but, in that event, what is to become of the Promise of the Seed? Yet, Abraham's faith is of such a quality, it is of such a working character, that he does not hesitate, "accounting that GOD was able to raise him up, even from the dead," as Hebrews xi. 19 tells us. James, in our passage, draws the inference, in verse 21, that Abraham was "justified by works"—his "works" consisted in his throwing himself upon GOD; it wasn't what he said, but what he did, that shewed the quality of his faith, and on account of which, therefore, he was justified. Yet, both Romans iv. and Galatians iii. assert most positively that he was justified by faith—let it be said again that the two statements are not contradictory, but complementary. By faith—yes; by works—yes; in fact, by a faith that works. Thus are we brought back once more to the conclusion that the apparent discrepancy is due to the fact that, while using the same word, they each give to it a different meaning; but in reality they are, of course, of one mind. Which is only what we should expect—seeing that they are both alike inspired, in their writing, by the same HOLY SPIRIT.

Then, there is Rahab—a strange and striking example of GOD'S sovereign exercise of His saving power. We turn for the story to Joshua ii., where, in verse 9, she says, "I know that the LORD hath given you the land." That was her faith: but once more we enquire, was it a Faith of Words merely, or was it a Faith of Works? Indubitably, the latter; for she shewed its living reality by what she did—by throwing in her lot with GOD, going over to His side in contrast to all the rest of the city; and then by sheltering herself behind the scarlet line. Thus, says James, was she "justified by works", verse 25; her "works" consisted in her throwing herself upon GOD. But her case is dealt with also in Hebrews xi., and there, in the 31st verse, it is said that it was "by faith [she] perished not". For the last time we say, there is no contradiction here. By faith—yes; by works—yes; in fact, by a faith that works.

By the way, have you noticed that whenever Rahab is mentioned in Scripture, she is always designated as "the harlot". It reminds one of Jeroboam, the son of Nebat, to whose name it is so frequently added that he "made Israel to sin"; and of Nicodemus, who, upon all his appearances on the sacred page is described as the man "that came to JESUS by night"—the poor man couldn't escape the stigma. There is, of course, always a reason for this pointed reiteration. In Rahab's case, it is, I think, not far to seek. I fancy it is that GOD would have us keep always in mind that, though she was saved, it was not for her own merit—she deserved nothing but judgment; she was "the harlot". Yet, by His own choice, GOD saved her. You, my reader, have not been, or will not be, saved by your own merit any more than she; you are "the sinner", as, according to the Greek, the publican of Luke xviii. 13 confessed himself—and therefore, "not by works of righteousness which we have done, but according to His mercy He saved us," Titus iii. 5.

This, then, is the nature of saving faith. It is (*a*) *A step* —not merely a statement; verses 15-6 shew how profitless is mere speech; but real, living, belief moves towards Him, takes a step, (*b*) *In the dark*—that is of the very nature of faith; we believe when we cannot understand, trust when we cannot trace, step out when we cannot see, (*c*) *On to a Rock*—though there seemed to be nothing, there proved to be He. Go back to my grocer's boy, and see what a splendid illustration he is of all this. This is how true faith works—and, consequently, how true faith saves.

It has now to be added, in conclusion (and perhaps its coming last will secure for it the emphasis that its importance demands) that to the "first work" of a live faith, of which we have been speaking, there will inevitably be added—again, if that faith be alive—the exhibition of "good works" ("good deeds", if you like) in the daily conduct: for example, the characteristic manners of a real Christian, the upright behaviour of a true child of God, the impulsive acts of a Christ-like nature, the earnest service of a consciously redeemed bond-slave. Such things will not of themselves procure our salvation, but they will follow if that salvation be of the right, live sort; as Paul says in Ephesians ii. 9-10, our salvation is "not *of* works . . . but *unto* good works"—God means them to follow, as the conclusion of that 10th verse shews, and as Titus ii. 14 explicitly states—"a . . . people zealous of good works." Good works, then, both James and Paul teach us, are to follow the "first work". We cannot close this study better than on the note of Titus iii. 8—"they which have believed . . . might be careful to maintain good works." How like James that sounds!

A SUBJECT THAT IS IN EVERYBODY'S MOUTH

JAMES III. 1-12

1 My brethren, be not many masters, knowing that we shall receive the greater condemnation.

2 For in many things we offend all. If any man offend not in word, the same *is* a perfect man, *and* able also to bridle the whole body.

3 Behold, we put bits in the horses' mouths, that they may obey us; and we turn about their whole body.

4 Behold also the ships, which though *they be* so great, and *are* driven of fierce winds, yet are they turned about with a very small helm, whithersoever the governor listeth.

5 Even so the tongue is a little member, and boasteth great things. Behold, how great a matter a little fire kindleth!

6 And the tongue *is* a fire, a world of iniquity: so is the tongue among our members, that it defileth the whole body, and setteth on fire the course of nature; and it is set on fire of hell.

7 For every kind of beasts, and of birds, and of serpents, and of things in the sea, is tamed, and hath been tamed of mankind:

8 But the tongue can no man tame; *it is* an unruly evil, full of deadly poison.

9 Therewith bless we God, even the Father; and therewith curse we men, which are made after the similitude of God.

10 Out of the same mouth proceedeth blessing and cursing. My brethren, these things ought not so to be.

11 Doth a fountain send forth at the same place sweet *water* and bitter?

12 Can the fig tree, my brethren, bear olive berries? either a vine, figs? so *can* no fountain both yield salt water and fresh.

A SUBJECT THAT IS IN EVERYBODY'S MOUTH

III. 1-12

It is, of course, the Tongue; and it is noteworthy that our writer has, within the restricted space of his brief Letter, so much to say upon the subject. Five times over he brings it up—in i. 19; 26; ii. 12; iv. 11; v. 12; in addition to this passage of to-day's study, when he deals with the matter at some length. It seems evident that what Matthew Henry calls "tongue-sins" were rather prevalent amongst these Christians. Would James find them any less common if he were to visit some of our churches to-day? Alas, there are few sins that more frequently, or more glaringly, besmirch and disfigure the fair figure of religion in this age. Let us, then, give earnest heed to the exhortations of this solemn paragraph.

I have said before that James is a master of illustration; and here, in order to drive home his teaching on this subject, he offers us no less than seven different pictures of the Tongue. These I propose to consider in groups, and the first two will shew us—

How the Tongue Guides Life

The "bit", of verse 3, is our first figure. Just a little instrument, but what helpful service it can render. The young horse—strong, and good to look at; champing and chafing at restriction; restive and restless; longing to be on the go—caring not much where, so long as he is moving; not of itself very capable of knowing which is the right, and best, way to go. The "bit" will regulate all that, and direct his fine energies into wise and useful channels.

What a picture is all this of our fine young life of to-day —every phrase of our description has its counterpart in their make-up and outlook. And just a little "bit" of a word can set the direction of their whole life for good— or for evil; just a touch may "turn about their whole body". Forgive two personal allusions. When I was about 17 years old, a young Christian, beginning to think of GOD's service, a then curate of Christ Church, Gipsy Hill, where I belonged, the Rev. J. L. Cobham, said to me one day, "Will you take a Sunday School class?" That was the last thing I wanted, for I had [then] no interest in children. However, if the present Archdeacon Cobham will forgive my publishing the dark secret, I had, in my heart of hearts, the profoundest admiration, and deepest affection, for him; and so I agreed to his suggestion. That night I prayed GOD to give me a love for children, and my prayer was instantly, and constantly, answered; and from that moment began all the work among children that has been my increasing delight. Just a word; just a "bit"— and it set the direction of much of my life. May I give another instance? One morning, some years ago, a young fellow, in business, came to see me. I knew him for a very keen man, whose life was destined for an ordinary business career. As he was leaving my study, I said to him, "When are you coming to be my curate?" We both smiled at the idea; for a life in the ministry had never occurred to him. Nevertheless, that word was as a "bit" to that young "horse"—if I may so irreverently designate the Rev. Richard Rees, now Vicar of Holy Trinity, Brompton, Chatham, after having served splendidly as curate in two important parishes (though, be it noted, not to me!) and as a chaplain in the Royal Air Force. I expect you could multiply such instances. What a "bit" the Tongue can be, to guide a young life.

The "helm", of verse 4, is another illustration of the

Tongue's influence. "The ships . . . so great" may perhaps be accounted not altogether unlike the lives of older folks, battling across life's ocean, often "driven of fierce winds" of the storms and tempests of trouble, wave after wave of misfortune breaking over them, not knowing where to find the harbour and haven of peace. How often, in such circumstances, has a word of good cheer, a word of sincere comfort, a word of simple testimony, been as a "helm" to guide the troubled soul to the "great calm" of the Saviour's blessing.

Yes, indeed, the Tongue has a great ministry of guidance to exercise; but, for all that, we are warned, in the first verse of our passage, "be not many masters"—that is, do not all rush to be teachers, as if it were something easy of accomplishment, and of little responsibility. On the contrary, those who take up the position of teacher, take upon themselves all the heavier burden, and will "receive the greater judgment". Besides, we are all prone to fall; and if a teacher fall, he is in danger of causing the taught to "offend"—with all the serious implications of such a situation, as outlined in Matthew xviii. 6f. Nowhere is the peril of failure more likely than in the realm of the Tongue; and in no other sphere is strength of character, and advancement in Christian grace, so evident. "If any man" —teacher, or anyone else—is victorious in this, he is, indeed, "a perfect man", a strong mature Christian, gloriously qualified to act the "bit" to younger lives, and the "helm" to those that are further on. But now let us consider the three illustrations that shew—

How the Tongue Harms Life

The "fire", of verse 5, comes first. What devastation it can work: "how great a forest a little fire kindleth". Only a spark, only a match—and very quickly a whole forest may be ablaze. The tongue can be equally destructive.

It may degenerate into "a world of iniquity"—the sum total of unrighteousness. There is no divine law that, in spirit if not in actual letter, it cannot break—this can be said neither of the hand, nor the eye, nor any other member but the tongue. Test that statement by the Ten Commandments—the spirit of every one of the Ten can be broken by the Tongue. "It defileth the whole body"—even as fire defiles with its smoke. It fires "the wheel of nature" (see Margin)—that is, the whole round of life. What an indictment—the whole of wickedness, in the whole of man, for the whole of life! Yes, "how great a forest". But will anyone say that this is an exaggeration? Certainly none who has ever seen how a hot, burning, word has started a conflagration in some individual, or in some community. Truly, the Tongue can be a veritable fire.

The "beast", of verse 7, comes next. What a beast the Tongue can be—in more senses than one! This is a very interesting account of the tameableness of creation. Beasts, of course, can be tamed, as any circus will demonstrate; birds, too, have been made very tame and friendly; serpents, also, have been schooled by music; but—fish! Well, Izaak Walton (and who should know more about fish?) quotes Pliny as telling how one of the Roman emperors had particular fish-ponds in which were fish that appeared and came when they were called by their special names! But take solemn note of this, that "the tongue can no man tame"—so wild a beast it can be. We shall get this wrong unless we remember to read that sentence with the emphasis upon the word "man": no man can tame it, but I know Someone Who can—I have seen Him do it. A blaspheming tongue has been so tamed by Him as to accustom itself gladly to speak the praises of God; a back-biting, scandal-mongering tongue has been so tamed that it has eschewed the expression of any but the kindliest sentiments; a lying tongue has been so tamed that it has earned a widespread reputation for speaking only the truth; a passionate tongue, used to explode in uncontrolled rage, has been so tamed as to utter kind and gentle words. Yes, these miracles of grace have been wrought on this "little member"; but without that taming touch of GOD, what a beast it can be!

The "poison", of verse 8, comes last in this lamentable series. The deadly drug does not need to be taken in large doses—a drop or two will suffice; and the tongue does not need to distil long speeches, it has but to drop a word, and the mischief is set afoot. Thus has a peace been ruined, thus has a reputation been blackened, thus has a friendship been embittered, thus has a mind been poisoned, thus has a life been blasted. Let a child's rhyme point the same moral—

"I lost a very little word, only the other day;
It was a very naughty word I had not meant to say.
But, then, it was not really lost—when from my lips it flew,
My little brother picked it up, and now he says it too!"

In such small unconsidered ways, as well as in the more designedly deliberate fashion, are minds and lives poisoned by a word, by the Tongue.

In the face of all that we have said, how needful is the prayer of Psalm cxli. 3, "Keep the door of my lips"—a request that might well become one of our regular morning petitions. Yet, we realise that the trouble is really lower down. Do you remember the story of Simon Magus, one of the "converts" of Philip's great Mission in Samaria—I suppose he really was a genuine convert, seeing that it is said that he "believed . . . and . . . was baptized". Anyhow, he subsequently committed a grievous sin of the Tongue; for when Peter and John came down from

Jerusalem and laid their hands on the converts, there were such remarkable results of the HOLY SPIRIT, that Simon actually offered to buy the secret. The point I want to stress here is, that Peter did not blame the Tongue, but went to the very root of the matter, and said, "Thy heart is not right in the sight of GOD," Acts viii. 21. The late renowned Dr. Parker, writing in a quite different connection, said, "It is in vain to attempt to tame the tongue until the heart has been subdued".

It is in the heart, therefore, that the healing work must be done—the heart, which is the peculiar province of the HOLY SPIRIT indwelling the believer; regulating the tongue, which is the immediate interest of the HOLY SPIRIT infilling the believer. It is not without deep significance that when He was outpoured at Pentecost, the visible sign of His arrival was the fiery Tongues; neither is it to be ignored that the first effect upon the apostles was that "they were all filled with the HOLY GHOST, and began to speak with other tongues," Acts ii. 4. It is probably your trouble, however, to know how to begin to speak properly with your own tongue—and this is apparently a problem that the HOLY SPIRIT is particularly concerned to tackle for you. If we seek day by day to be filled with the SPIRIT, He will assume the control of our tongue. This is good news—isn't it?—when we come to understand how the tongue harms life. But now let us turn to James' last two pictures, and note their suggestion of—

HOW THE TONGUE BLESSES LIFE

The "fountain", of verse 11, is one. What blessed refreshment the Tongue can bring to a heart that is weary—just a word only, but what tonic-water it can be. Of course, the absurd thing is that an uncontrolled tongue can be this at one time, and just the opposite at another—alternating "salt water and fresh" as verse 12 says. No ordinary fountain could exhibit such contrariness; and even so, as Matthew Henry says, "True religion will not admit of contradictions". Let us pray that there may be no inconsistency of tongue about us, but that this fountain's water my be uniformly "sweet". If it has been otherwise, let us plead that the "bitter" be made sweet. Marah's bitter waters "were made sweet" by Moses, in Exodus xv. 23-7, because "the LORD shewed him a tree"; and it will be the beneficent efficacy of that other Tree of Acts x. 39 and 1 Peter ii. 24 that the HOLY SPIRIT will use to sweeten all our flow of speech. Of our all-too-frequent inconsistencies of tongue the passage says, "My brethren, these things ought not so to be", and over every "ought not" of Scripture you may, in triumphant faith, write "need not"; and over that again you may put "shall not". There is never any need to do what we ought not to do—because, as we have seen, the HOLY SPIRIT is ever ready to enable us to enter into the releasing and enabling power of the Cross; and so, as Romans vi. 14 promises, "Sin *shall* not have dominion over you"—ought not, need not, and therefore shall not. And this applies to all tongue-sin!

The "tree", of verse 12, is the concluding illustration. What blessed nourishment the Tongue can bring to a life that is weak. The old word of Proverbs xv. 4 is still true, that "a wholesome tongue is a tree of life"; and many a time, perhaps in your own experience, it has been verified—somebody has said the word that was food to your soul. May we all, in our turn, be "trees of righteousness, the planting of the LORD, that He might be glorified", as in Isaiah lxi. 3; and, to that end, may we continually "take root downward", the secret root-work of the quiet time with GOD, and "bear fruit upward", the open life before our fellows, as we read in Isaiah xxxvii. 31. Our great English poet speaks of "tongues in trees": here are trees in tongues.

When we feel ill and out-of-sorts, and go to consult a doctor, one of the first things he will probably say is, "Let me look at your tongue". What an index it is of the health—either physical, or spiritual. "If a man offend not in word", if his tongue is healthy, "the same is a perfect man, and able also to bridle the whole body", as our second verse says. May the HOLY SPIRIT, then, be so given control in us, that He may be as "the Governor" of verse 4, doing in us, and for us, whatsoever He "listeth", that our Tongue may be continually employed in "blessing" GOD, and in blessing, not "cursing", man.

A thorough-going Christian may be recognised by his Tongue. You will recall Peter's giving himself away, "Surely thou also art one of them; for thy speech bewrayeth thee", Matthew xxvi. 73. The Master's disciples, with the one exception of Judas Iscariot, were Galileans; and it was Peter's accent that betrayed him, he had the characteristic North Country "burr". He was recognised as one of JESUS' disciples by the test of the Tongue. Poor Peter, in his hour of failure, resented it; but we may gladly welcome it, if by the manner of our speech, and by the use of our tongue, we betray ourselves to the world as one of His.

"O that it might be said of me,
Surely thy speech bewrayeth thee,
Thou hast been with JESUS of Galilee,
With JESUS of Galilee."

WISE AND OTHERWISE

JAMES III. 13-18

13 Who *is* a wise man and endued with knowledge among you? let him shew out of a good conversation his works with meekness of wisdom.

14 But if ye have bitter envying and strife in your hearts, glory not, and lie not against the truth.

15 This wisdom descendeth not from above, but *is* earthly, sensual, devilish.

16 For where envying and strife *is,* there *is* confusion and every evil work.

17 But the wisdom that is from above is first pure, then peaceable, gentle, *and* easy to be intreated, full of mercy and good fruits, without partiality, and without hypocrisy.

18 And the fruit of righteousness is sown in peace of them that make peace.

WISE AND OTHERWISE

III. 13-18

It is an extraordinary thing that this paragraph is addressed to Christian people, and even to believers of the first Christian era. There seems to be little doubt that those early saints suffered from the same human failings and weaknesses as we do, and that they were subject to the very same temptations to sin. When we read the passage thoughtfully through, it seems that it would be impossible for some of the dreadful things mentioned to be present in a Christian assembly, or in a Christian life. Well—so it was; and so, alas, it still is. It would appear that there were many known to James—many, perhaps, of those "teachers" to whom he referred in the earlier part of this chapter—who professed to be very wise in the things of God and consequently well able to be instructors of others. It is for this reason that he turns to a discussion of—

The Truly Wise

He opens it by asking a question: "Who is a wise man and endued with knowledge among you?" Many of the commentators imagine those "teachers" as answering the enquiry, with some alacrity, and certainly with plenty of confidence, "We are"! They undoubtedly thought this of themselves. Let it be said that there are many who are full of knowledge while being empty of wisdom. On the other hand, there are some who, while possessing little knowledge, yet have much wisdom. The writer's question visualises those who enjoy both the gifts. The distinction between the two is rather happily put in the following lines of Cowper—

> "Knowledge and wisdom, far from being one,
> Have oft-times no connection. Knowledge dwells
> In heads replete with thoughts of other men;
> Wisdom in minds attentive to their own.
> Knowledge, a rude unprofitable mass,
> The mere materials with which wisdom builds,
> Till smoothed and squared, and fitted to its place,
> Does but encumber whom it seems to enrich.
> Knowledge is proud that he has learned so much;
> Wisdom is humble that he knows no more."

So, then, is the really wise man sought, and two tokens are offered by the which he shall be recognised.

If really wise—it will be shewn in his life. Not by what he says—those "teachers" could say so much—but by what he does, and is. "Let him shew out of a good conversation his works", says verse 13. Strange how that word "conversation" has altered its meaning! It now means Talk; it used to mean Walk—the manner of life, the quality of conduct. The passage lays it down that it's better to walk than talk. Our writer has been dealing at some length with Talk in the previous verses; but now he proceeds to say that the evidence of true wisdom lies, rather, in Walk—"a good conversation": an upright, sincere, holy and godly life. Moreover—

If really wise—it will be shewn in his bearing. "With meekness of wisdom"—it is the genitive of possession: the meekness that belongs to wisdom. That is not true wisdom which is not meek. It is the difficult quality that stands for the absence of self-assertiveness, for the absence, indeed, of self altogether. It would not be far from the truth to say that Meekness means, "Not I"; and Christian Meekness adds, "But CHRIST", as Galatians ii. 20 teaches us. I have called it a "difficult" quality, for let no one suppose that Meekness is Weakness. Any who are disposed to entertain that notion should try to be meek for a week! In any case, this trait of meekness ("modesty", as Dr. Moffatt translates it) is part of the very essence of the character of true wisdom; by it the difference between the spurious and the real can be readily detected. These are, as we have said, the two tokens of wisdom—one, our behaviour; and two, our demeanour. Let us stay a moment, and examine our own selves, that we may know whether, or not, we are among GOD's wise men or wise women.

The writer will enlarge upon this type of wisdom presently, at the close of the paragraph; but, meanwhile, he turns aside for a bit, that he may teach by vivid contrast, to consider—

THE WORLDLY WISE

"This wisdom"—yes, there is such a wisdom: it exercises its own power, scores its own successes; but it is sharply distinguishable from that which we have just been examining. The difference is set out here in verses 14-16, and is shewn to consist in three things.

Its motives are all wrong. "Bitter envying and strife in your hearts"—it is sad beyond words to have to acknowledge that some supposedly Christian service is rendered for motives even as low as these; a horrid jealousy of others who are held in high repute, a wrangling partisan spirit. It is quite possible to enjoy a very considerable measure of success in the work—if the skill is there, if the tact is there, if the personality is there, if the enthusiasm is there; but if the motive is self-seeking, or party faction, the success is of little avail. That is why James says, "Glory not". It is verily a "lie . . . against the truth" to acclaim such base-motived service and success as the real thing! How refreshing (yes, and how searching) it is to turn from all this to the all-inclusive motive that set Paul going, and that kept him going, in the work of the Master, however hard the road, however high the cost. It is in 2 Corinthians v. 14 that he lets us into his secret: "The love of CHRIST constraineth us". Another unfortunate aspect of this worldly wisdom is that—

Its characteristics are all wrong. "Earthly, sensual, devilish"—what a description; and what a tragedy that this is the type of wisdom, the sort of reasoning, that dictates the activity of some of us Christians, and some of our churches. All too often there is no other, or higher, contribution to the discussion of ways and means than what could be made by any sensible man of the world; the measure of success is wholly worldly, the method of seeking it is equally so. A great many of us are content with such a miserably low level—our Christian attainment, our Christian experience, scarcely deserve the name of Christian at all; we so rarely get beyond the "earthly". Moreover, the wisdom that inspires such service is "sensual"—or, "natural", as your Margin tells you. There is nothing spiritual about it; indeed, your observation might lead you to suppose that the man had never been supernaturally "born again" into the spiritual life at all, so nearly does he behave, and speak, and think, to his old "natural" sinful self. The really "natural" man is all at sea about spiritual things, as Paul teaches us in 1 Corinthians ii. 14: "The natural man receiveth not the things of the SPIRIT of GOD: for they are foolishness unto him: neither can he know them, because they are spiritually discerned". The low-level Christian is not now actually a "natural" man, but he acts as if he were. In his following chapter Paul calls him a "carnal" man (iii. 1)—his outlook is physical, temporal, material; his wisdom is all wrong. Indeed, to such depths can it lead him, into such difficulties can it betray him, that it may truthfully be described as "devilish". Verily, the devil has a wisdom of his own —but what a wisdom; what motives, what characteristics. Moreover,

Its results are all wrong. "Confusion, and every evil work"—such is the issue of so much of this worldly wisdom. Its promises are so fair; but its performances all too readily leave the circle of believers, or the individual Christian, in a state of tumult and unrest, and pave the way for all kinds of unfortunate evil. What havoc has been wrought in the church by "Mr. Worldly-Wiseman"—the rising tide of spiritual revival has been stayed, the holy task of soul-winning has been impaired, the commanding voice of Christian testimony has been silenced, the growing experience of blessed intimacy with God has been arrested; yes, and many more deplorable effects have ensued when worldly wisdom has been allowed its way. These three verses have made sad reading; yet, they are very salutary. It is as Dr. Dale said: "The passage stands on the pages of this Epistle as an awful warning to the Church of every generation". We all need to hearken to its solemn words, and to hearken not in any spirit of judgment of others, but of earnest examination of our own hearts, to discover whether we are, by any chance, swayed by the worldly-wise views and aims and means that we have been discussing. And then, what a joy to turn, with our Epistle, to—

The Other Wise

"The wisdom that is from above"—which he introduced to us in verse 13, and to which he returns now in amplification, in verses 17 and 18. It is an exquisite picture that the Holy Spirit leads him to draw for us, and we shall look into the features of the portrait with great delight, and with earnest desire that such wisdom may be ours.

"*Pure.*" It is that before anything else. The word

has a significance all its own. That great New Testament scholar, the late Bishop Westcott, in his commentary on the First Epistle of John, when expounding 1 John iii. 3, says that this word "suggests the notion of shrinking from contamination, of a delicate sensibility to pollution of any kind". And that is, indeed, a matter of "first" and fundamental importance. It is impossible to exaggerate the value of a sensitive conscience. The conscience is not, in itself, the voice of GOD, though it is manifestly intended to act as a medium for that voice, and if properly trained and exercised in the Word, does succeed, as we obey its decisions, in conveying to us the Mind and Ruling of GOD upon matters in dispute—"accusing or . . . excusing", as Romans ii. 15 has it. Milton calls it "the Umpire of the Soul"; but, alas, you can have a bad umpire, whose decisions are not reliable. Some of the ghastliest crimes in history have been done in the name of conscience! Let us, then, pray that, by educating it in Holy Scripture, we may ever retain the finely adjusted conscience, and ever be "first pure" in our wisdom. And then—

"*Peaceable.*" Not quarrelsome, or contentious, but always seeking the peaceful way. Sometimes it will become inescapably necessary to fight—in some doctrinal, or practical, issue; but even then to have the peaceable spirit, that only fights in the interest of peace. Some Christians are aggressive even in promoting peace, a natural pugnacity seems to spoil all their efforts. I wonder if you have come across that sentence of Cardinal Newman's in reply to Pusey—"You have discharged your olive branch from a catapult". That is how not to do it.

"*Gentle.*" That is, "forbearing"—the complete absence of harsh criticism of others, the quality that is always ready to make allowances, always inventive in finding excuses—not for oneself, but for others. How attractive —and, withal, how effective—a feature this is in the character of "the wisdom that is from above". Next comes—

"*Easy to be intreated.*" There is a form of obstinacy which, having said a thing, having taken a line, refuses in any circumstances to alter—no matter what added arguments are adduced, what new light is available. That is an attitude quite foreign to Wisdom. There should always be a certain yieldingness about us—a readiness to consider another view of the case, a readiness to admit that [even] we might be wrong. "Conciliatory" is Dr. Moffatt's word for this.

"*Full of mercy and good fruits.*" That form of so-called wisdom which is spoken of as "a knowledge of the world" is often apt to be cynical and hard towards the misfortunes of others. True wisdom is so different from that; in its contemplation of men, it bears with their sins, pities their sorrows, feels for their sufferings. Moreover, this merciful regard is fruitful in practice: it is not of that sterile sort which is described in verses 15 and 16 of the previous chapter. It moves among men with a sympathy that is sufficiently genuine to try to be practical.

"*Without partiality.*" Or, as the Revised Version has it, "without variance". He is no trimmer of his sails, to catch the passing breeze; rather is he a man of fixed principle. He is not a person of bewildering changeability, whom you never know quite how to take; he is utterly dependable, you always know where you are with him. He is not the objectionable type of being who has one set of manners for the rich, and another—or, more truthfully, no manners at all—for the poor; against such "respect of persons" James has, in chapter two, already warned us. There is about this Man of Wisdom that true consistency which is such an ornament.

"*Without hypocrisy.*" Here is something that we all understand—and all admire. Worldly wisdom often makes a hypocrite of a man—causing him to fawn and flatter;

but the other-wise are never caught that way. In thought and word and deed they are transparently honest and sincere. What an alluring catalogue of virtues. And what a "harvest of righteousness" will accrue when such a Wisdom, such a Life, is "sown" among men.

One's mind goes back, in closing, to that word of Paul's in Colossians iv. 5: "Walk in wisdom toward them that are without." We have seen throughout this study how great are the blessings of the Wise Walk to our own selves; and how much it contributes towards our helpful influence upon our fellow believers. Spare a thought now, as we finish, for "them that are without"—the people of the world, who do not know the Saviour. If the kind of wisdom that James has been delineating for us were to characterise our behaviour "toward" them, and in their sight, what a mighty impression it would make; if all the Christians were to live thus the Wise Life before the world, a veritable Revival might soon sweep through the land. Wherefore, let us make the prayer of i. 5 our own!

A FEW HOME TRUTHS

JAMES IV. 1-12

1 From whence *come* wars and fightings among you? *come they* not hence, *even* of your lusts that war in your members?

2 Ye lust, and have not: ye kill, and desire to have, and cannot obtain: ye fight and war, yet ye have not, because ye ask not.

3 Ye ask, and receive not, because ye ask amiss, that ye may consume *it* upon your lusts.

4 Ye adulterers and adulteresses, know ye not that the friendship of the world is enmity with God? Whosoever therefore will be a friend of the world is the enemy of God.

5 Do ye think that the scripture saith in vain, The spirit that dwelleth in us lusteth to envy?

6 But he giveth more grace. Wherefore he saith, God resisteth the proud, but giveth grace unto the humble.

7 Submit yourselves therefore to God. Resist the devil, and he will flee from you.

8 Draw nigh to God, and he will draw nigh to you. Cleanse *your* hands, *ye* sinners; and purify *your* hearts, *ye* double minded.

9 Be afflicted, and mourn, and weep: let your laughter be turned to mourning, and *your* joy to heaviness.

10 Humble yourselves in the sight of the Lord, and he shall lift you up.

11 Speak not evil one of another, brethren. He that speaketh evil of *his* brother, and judgeth his brother, speaketh evil of the law, and judgeth the law: but if thou judge the law, thou art not a doer of the law, but a judge.

12 There is one lawgiver, who is able to save and to destroy: who art thou that judgest another?

A FEW HOME TRUTHS

IV. 1-12

JAMES is still writing in that practical vein which has so markedly characterised all that he has so far said. As before, he is more concerned with behaviour than with profession; and, led of the SPIRIT, he offers here a few home truths on four matters that have proved a constant trouble both among companies of Christians, and in individual Christians. And first—

ABOUT WRANGLING

He deals with this matter in the opening three verses of the chapter, where we note—

A serious condition—"wars and fightings". What he says does not refer to national conflicts, although a good deal may certainly apply to it; rather is he thinking about personal squabbles, disputes, discords. Such are described as existing (*a*) "among you"—that is, in the churches, and (*b*) "in your members"—or, in the individuals. Evidently, there was a great deal of bickering going on; and I am afraid that it has not yet ceased, after all these nearly nineteen-hundred years. But, what a terribly serious condition to be in—for the Church, or for the Christian! What a tragic weakening of the testimony to the world outside! Of course, it is all accounted for by—

A poisoned spring—"your lusts . . . ye lust". They are different words in the original: the first might be translated "pleasures", and the other rendered "longings"—that is, longings after those pleasures. At the bottom of all this unrest, this widespread bellicosity, lay the eager desire of self-pleasing, the yearning of self-love. Think of some of the forms that it takes, and note how these things are responsible for so much of the strife and clashing that spoil so much of our Christianity—love of money, what a prolific cause of enmities; love of display, to appear in a good and important light amongst our fellows; love of power, that we may gratify our greed, if need be at the expense of another; love of pre-eminence, the pitiable reason for many a fight, and especially pitiful when it occurs, as sometimes it does, between Christians. We remember that not very pleasant person Diotrephes, "who loveth to have the pre-eminence", as 3 John 9 tells us, who loved it so dearly, clung to it so tenaciously, that he even refused to acknowledge the Apostle of Love, lest his own position and authority should come to be challenged. This "lust" for the pre-eminence, what havoc it has wrought in some churches, and in the hearts and characters of some Christians—what bitter opposition it has engendered amongst some who should have been "of the same mind in the LORD", Philippians iv. 2. This clash of selves on the part of those two keen women might have wrecked the peace and the testimony of the whole Philippian church. Thank GOD, by the power of His indwelling, these "lusts" of ours can be put right—not only the effects, but the causes, not only the symptoms, but the disease. Writing to those same Philippians, in ii. 13, Paul shews that He can deal, not only with the Deeds, but with the Desires—"GOD . . worketh in you both to will, and to do, of His good pleasure": not only to do it, you see, but to will, to want to do it. That is the root of the matter—the desire, the longing, the "lust", to recur to the word of the passage. Yes, there is—

A better way—after all their fighting, what had they got? Even if they secured the thing, they found it illusory—it did not bring them the satisfaction they hoped for. "Ye have not". Why? Because they had eschewed the better way—"ye ask not". Let us repeat, it is Christian people whose conduct is here under review; so it is legitimate to say that wrestling with GOD is so much better than wrangling with men. The point in dispute: don't argue about it, don't wrangle over it, tackle it in the Prayer Way. But, of course, we must again emphasize that the motive, the "lust", must be adjusted to the Will of GOD—not according to our wish, but "His good pleasure". Anything other than this will spell failure in the prayer method—"ye ask, and receive not, because ye ask amiss, that ye may consume it upon your [own] lusts", your own desires and longings, and pleasures: which bring us back to the same old trouble, the same bad old poisoned spring. To sum up, it would secure the incoming of a delightful atmosphere of peace into our Christian life if only all disputes were referred to prayer, all discords referred to prayer, all desires referred to prayer—asking GOD, instead of attacking others. And now for some more Home Truths on another Troubler of the Church—

ABOUT WORLDLINESS

This difficult problem is dealt with in verses 4-5; and very arresting is the manner in which it is there handled. To begin with, the writer uses—

A terrible name—"ye adulterers and adulteresses". The allusion would be thoroughly familiar to the readers, for they were Jewish Christians, and, like James himself, would have a pretty good acquaintance with the Old Testament Scriptures. They would know their Book of Hosea, whose whole prophecy was coloured by the theme that Israel was the Wife of JEHOVAH; they would know their fifty-fourth chapter of Isaiah, whose fifth verse declares "thy Maker is thy Husband"; and they would recall how often the sin of idolatry is spoken of as the crime of adultery—Israel broke her solemn vows. In the New Testament, the personnel has changed, but the parable remains. Now it is the Church —the body of all faithful, or believing, people—that is conceived as being in the privileged position. In that glorious day of "the marriage supper", the church will become "the Lamb's wife", Revelation xxi. 9; until that day, she is His bride, being got ready by the HOLY SPIRIT for the Bridegroom. Not idolatry now, but worldliness is looked upon as the bride's unfaithfulness—they who, as Christians, and part of His bride, are espoused to CHRIST [Note 2 Corinthians xi. 2f.] must not go flirting with the world, His rival. That word introduces us to the next point here—

An awful position—"the enemy of GOD". It is dreadful to contemplate the possibility of a believer placing himself in such a position—"enemy of GOD", "enemies of the cross of CHRIST", says Philippians iii. 18. Such are they who would be the friends of the world. I take "the world" to be whatever is (actively) hostile, or (passively) inimical, to GOD and His cause. (*a*) There are worldly Things—most of them not deliberately anti-GOD, but incidentally so, and effectually so, because they spoil our spiritual experience, retard our spiritual growth, vitiate our spiritual appetite, threaten our spiritual influence. We may, alas, cause others to stumble by doing things which to us may be no danger, but which to them may lead to sad enslavement. Such things might be "lawful" for me, but they would not be "expedient"—to use Paul's distinction, in 1 Corinthians vi. 12; x. 23—and therefore, because of their baneful influence on those others, I will not do them, as the apostle determines, for example, in 1 Corinthians viii. 13. The effect any of these things would have on me, if I did them; the effect they would have on others, if they saw me doing them—constitute them as "worldly" things, which it would be disloyalty to GOD to continue. (b) There are worldly People—often gifted, charming, upright, kind, but who are entirely god-less. "GOD is not in all his thoughts", as Psalm x. 4 has it. While remaining friendly towards such, we must not have them for our friends—we should find ourselves almost automatically lowering our standards in our desire not to embarrass them; their whole spirit is foreign, their outlook alien. We must not make friends of God's enemies. This is further pressed home by—

A remarkable statement—"the SPIRIT that dwelleth in us lusteth to envy". Nowhere, I think, does the Scripture say that, in so many words; but it does say it in effect. Moreover, it is not said "in vain": it is not an empty, meaningless statement, it is the expression of a real, and great, truth. You will observe that I have used a capital "S" for SPIRIT. Some expositors think that it is referring simply to the human spirit that dwells in our bodies; but personally I follow the majority of the commentators in holding that the HOLY SPIRIT is meant. I do so principally because the description of the SPIRIT is, so far as I remember, never used of man's spirit, while it is the exact delineation of GOD'S SPIRIT in a score of places—in Romans viii. 11, for instance. What a glorious truth it is, and what infinite possibilities it opens out, that, if we are Christians at all—however weak, however unsatisfactory, however young in the faith—the HOLY SPIRIT of GOD actually does indwell us. Paul was astonished that the Corinthian Christians were ignorant of the fact, 1 Corinthians vi. 19, and suggests that this ignorance was the explanation of the sad failure, and low level, of their lives. Well—have *we* grasped the truth? But, in what sense does He "lust to envy"—or desire jealously? You remember how, in Exodus xx. 5; xxxiv. 14, and other passages, He discloses Himself as "a jealous GOD": but, how so? Why, this is the jealousy of love, that covets the whole of our love and that cannot brook our coquetting with the world, His rival. J. B. Mayor's translation of this phrase brings out this same interpretation—he puts it, "jealously yearns for the entire devotion of the heart". How grand to be so loved; and how unworthy to squander any part of our love elsewhere than on Him—away, then, with Worldliness! And now—

ABOUT CONCEIT

Such is the subject upon which James next offers a few home truths, and he deals with the matter in verses 6*b*-10 of our passage. Wrangling and worldliness are so likely to minister to our self-esteem, to foster in us a good conceit of ourselves; yet the verses indicate that—

There is little to justify Conceit—"in the sight of the LORD". However they may be rated by their fellows, whatever may be their own opinion of themselves, GOD has them in very low esteem. (*a*) "Sinners," He calls them, whose "hands", typical of their fighting, wrangling ways, need to be cleansed. (*b*) "Double minded," He names them, whose "hearts", typical of their love, need to be purified of their Worldliness, that unworthy division of their affection, part for GOD, and part for His enemy. What room is there for conceit in those whom GOD has, in very faithfulness, to describe with such opprobrious epithets? On the other hand—

There is much to commend Humility—apart altogether from the deep appropriateness of such an attitude towards our Almighty and Holy GOD, see here but two results that flow from this lovely grace. (*a*) "GOD . . . nigh"—could anything be more blessed than to have "GOD *nigh*" to us? The glorious possibilities of service, and of fellowship, that lie in such nearness, are beyond price. Well, "the proud", as verse 6 tells us, GOD "*resisteth*"—that is, puts away from Him, keeps at a distance: make no mistake about it, no proud Christian is living close to GOD! But, "the humble" are given the privilege of this "grace", this undeserved benefit, this sweet secret of joy. Many results flow from such a demeanour; one other is mentioned here (*b*) "He shall lift you up", verse 10. Instead of the "heady" and dangerous exaltation of the proud, here is promised the true elevation to all that GOD counts high; and, in this sense of the words, the Lower the Higher!

Well, this is GOD's purpose for us. Don't resist GOD—"resist the devil"—that Antagonist who rules the World, by all means—"and he will flee from you"; but "submit to GOD"—and He will "draw near" to you. Happy the Christian who has learnt to be done with every vestige of Conceit, and to "walk humbly" with his GOD, as Micah vi. 8 directs him. And now, one more trouble is to be considered. James has something to say—

ABOUT CRITICISM

The two closing verses are given to this grave fault. Let us be quite clear that there are occasions on which, circumstances in which, it is not only permissible, but even necessary, to exercise a certain judgment of others—those who occupy positions of responsibility, those who are asked to give advice to, or concerning, people, those to whom application is made for references, all such are, of course, bound to judge, and to pronounce judgment. This is not the kind of thing that James has in mind, but that harsh uncharitable spirit that is for ever finding fault with other people—whether to their face, or behind their back: generally, I am afraid, the latter. This is a great disturbance to the peace of the Christian community, and it is often most cruel in its results. Unfortunately, it is a sin we are all of us very liable to.

James gives us four reasons why we should seek help from GOD to abstain from the practice. (1) *Because you are brethren*—"speak not evil one of another, brethren . . . his brother . . . his brother," verse 11. How good it would be if we could get more of the brotherly attitude among Christians, more of the spirit of fellowship, more of the sense of the family. I do love that bit in Galatians vi. 10 which says, "let us do good unto all men, especially unto them who are of the household of faith": kind to everybody, but especially so, of course, to our fellow-believers. This rule would sweep away, at one stroke, the horrid stigma of criticism which prevails in too many Christian circles. (2) *Because you are judging the law itself*—which, by not keeping, you are, in effect, criticising. That seems to be the meaning of verse 11. (3) *Because GOD is Himself the Lawgiver and the Judge*—it is with Him that we all have to do. Both the critic and the criticised must themselves be judged of Him, so it ill becomes either to assume the judge's rôle. (4) *Because, in any case, you are a fine one to judge.* In the Greek language, one of the ways of emphasising a word is to give it the first place in the sentence, when normally it would appear later: in this 12th verse, the word that is written first is "thou" and the sentence should therefore be stressed in reading, "Who art THOU that judgest another?" In other words, "You are the last person to be judging others, seeing that you yourself are so open to criticism"! So, on all grounds, it would be well to drop this bad habit of Criticism, wouldn't it? Yes; but it is a habit hard to cure—how can it be done? Wrangling, too—and Worldliness, also—and Conceit, as well. We have heard these Home Truths, and they have very likely brought conviction to us all—certainly to the writer; but, again we ask, How put things right?

Well, there is one little bit of our passage which I have not yet dealt with, and which I have deliberately left to the last: it is at the beginning of verse 6—"But He giveth more grace". We can't, "but He" can. The greater the difficulty, the greater the opportunity, the greater the weakness—the "more grace" He gives. As Dr. R. W. Dale put it, "The loftier His commands the larger his bounty". On the coins of GOD's currency amongst men, there are, of course, two sides—on one side is a Precept, the reverse is a Promise; and neither is ever, as on material coins, worn away. Thus it is that, in the words of Exodus xviii. 23, "If . . . GOD command thee . . . thou shalt be able to . . ."

"D. V."

JAMES IV. 13-17

13 Go to now, ye that say, To day or to morrow we will go into such a city, and continue there a year, and buy and sell, and get gain:

14 Whereas ye know not what *shall be* on the morrow. For what *is* your life? It is even a vapour, that appeareth for a little time, and then vanisheth away.

15 For that ye *ought* to say, If the Lord will, we shall live, and do this, or that.

16 But now ye rejoice in your boastings: all such rejoicing is evil.

17 Therefore to him that knoweth to do good, and doeth *it* not, to him it is sin.

"D. V."

IV. 13—17

OUR Epistle turns now to address a special exhortation to the business men amongst its readers. I wonder if you approve of mixing Religion and Business? James heartily believed in mixing Religion with every aspect and department of life—he would regard any part of human activity which could not admit Religion as something wholly illegitimate for a Christian. A customer went into a shop one day during the lunch hour, and suggested some shady trick of accommodation to the young assistant on the specious plea that his master was out. But the tempter was crushed by the firm, but polite, rejoinder, "Excuse me, but my Master is always in"! Note that capital "M". How James would have enjoyed that example of mixing Religion and Business. Or—that delightful pair of testimonies concerning Joseph, in Genesis xxxix. 2-3—(*a*) "The LORD was with Joseph", and (*b*) "His master saw that the LORD was with him". There was a something about the manner in which the young fellow did his work that forced his employer to recognise GOD'S presence and power with him. Religion and Business again! James was too keen a student of his Old Testament to have missed that illustration. Of course, there have been those who mixed the two who have resorted to such behaviour, so inconsistent with their loud, and sometimes sanctimonious, professions, that they have sickened their employees, alienated their clients, and, worst of all, dishonoured their LORD. The whole tenor of this Epistle indicates that its writer would have no shred of sympathy for such.

These whom James addresses, mostly, perhaps, Jews of the Eastern Dispersion, sojourners in Syria, Arabia, and Mesopotamia, included within their number, as Dr. David Smith has pointed out, many engaged in the lucrative traffic in ivory and ebony, purple dyes, wines, cedar-wood, gold, pearls, emeralds, agates, silk and embroidery. Hence, in the next chapter, he will have some special straight words to say to the "rich men" amongst them (v. 1). But first he has something to say to all the business men there —and, indeed, here; "for whatsoever things were written aforetime were written for our learning", as Romans xv. 4 says. So, in our passage we are bidden to consider—

A MAN'S DIARY

It is interesting to observe how he maps out his list of engagements. (*a*) *He chooses his time*—"to-day or to-morrow". But in reality the choice is not his to make. What can he know about to-morrow, or whether, even, there will be a to-morrow? He had better bear in mind, and take to heart, those lines on a Sundial—

> "Time was—thou hast not, canst not it recall.
> Time will be—is not, may not be at all.
> Time is—thou hast it, use it best of all."

Just this portion of to-day we can reckon on, but certainly not to-morrow. Then we observe that (*b*) *He selects his spot*—"We will go into such a city". Yet how many a turn of fortune might forbid his journey, or prevent his arrival. Anyhow, he makes his arrangements and fixes his appointments, and when he has exhausted the possibilities of that city, he will doubtless move on to the next. So his route is planned well ahead. For (*c*) *He limits his stay*—"continue there a year". The word translated "continue" is used four times in this passage, and in the three other than this, it is rendered "do"—this business man does not propose merely to "continue" for that year, to stagnate, to let the grass grow under his feet; no, he will busily occupy his time, he will "do" there for a year, and, in all likelihood, he will do very well, since (*d*) *He plans his doings*—"buy and sell", never dreaming for a moment that he might be so stricken with illness that he cannot carry on, or that he might find a paucity of merchants ready to trade with him. As to this latter, perhaps we may presume that he is so keen a business man that he would never have chosen that city if he had not been perfectly well assured that there was plenty for him to "do" there for a whole year. And so (*e*) *He reckons his profits*—"get gain". He hasn't begun yet; but, you see, he shares, even thus early, what has become the habitual business acumen and optimism of his race.

But, is not all this thoroughly commendable? If business is to go on at all, surely there must be planning ahead, and careful and intelligent organisation? Oh yes, James has no intention of blessing an unbusinesslike opportunism, a slack and slovenly way of conducting affairs. That would be clean contrary to the whole teaching of the New Testament concerning what we call the secular side of life. Colossians iii. 23 teaches the humblest workers, "Whatsoever ye do, do it heartily, as to the LORD, and not [merely] unto men"; while Romans xii. 11 bids us be "not slothful in business". GOD is ever a GOD of order: that is the very first representation of Him that we get in Holy Writ, and that is the delightsome impression of Him that we always get after a few minutes with a microscope. He would not approve of disorder in any walk, or work, of life; He would not inspire James to say one word that would encourage Christians to conduct their business in a haphazard way. It is indeed praiseworthy that they should proceed in the orderly and sensible fashion just described. The trouble was different from that—the fact is, there was a note that was completely absent from all this planning; this business man's Diary was spoilt, not by an inclusion, but by an omission. Before we discuss that, let us consider—

A Man's Day

His present day—"what shall be on the morrow", cannot be predicted with complete accuracy. It really does not do to put off till to-morrow the doing of anything that is deemed important. In this connection, there are two texts that I often link up together: One is in Proverbs iii. 28, and runs, "Say not . . . to morrow"; the other is in Hebrews iii. 7, which says, "The Holy Ghost saith, To day". With certain natures, it is so easy to put things off. In the fundamental decisions of life, it is fatal to procrastinate; in so many less important matters, it is at least folly to procrastinate. Browning has a word relative to the former category, which he puts into the mouth of that Rabbi Ben Karshook, who "taught babes in grace their grammar"; he says—

"'Would a man 'scape the rod?'
Rabbi Ben Karshook saith,
'See that he turn to God
The day before his death'.

'Ay could a man inquire
When it shall come!' I say,
The Rabbi's eye shoots fire—
'Then let him turn to-day'."

His present day is all that he can be quite certain of; not even to-morrow can be reckoned on, for the Book tells us, in Proverbs xxvii. 1, "Boast not thyself of to-morrow; for thou knowest not what a day may bring forth", so frail is—

His life's day—"what is your life?" It is so brief a thing—"a vapour", the steam issuing from a kettle's spout, there a moment, gone the next. That is GOD'S picture of its duration. You may say that you have thirty or forty years yet to live. Have you? What a little time; it will soon be gone. But, have you? Perhaps; perhaps not. The finger of Death may quite unexpectedly touch you, and life's Day will be suddenly done. These are times when such things are happening all around us. As I write these words, it is only a few hours since that a broken-hearted father said to me "I was building such castles in the air"—his little son, only ten months old, had been instantaneously killed by a shell. Yes—"it is even a vapour". Maybe not Death, but the Second Coming of CHRIST, will end your life's day, for that blessed event might so well be nearer than we sometimes think.

Yet, let it once again be said that the transitoriness of man's Day is no reason for him to eschew a planned life. The great evangelist, George Whitefield, whose life was crammed full of engagements to preach the Gospel here, there, and everywhere, was asked what he would do if he knew for certain that the Saviour would return in three days' time. He produced his Diary, wherein were recorded all his preaching appointments and, opening it at the appropriate days, he passed the book to his questioner and said, "That is what I should do". That is, of course, the right attitude—to plan ahead, to go through the plan so far as may be, but to be ready at any moment for the vapour to "vanish away", as verse 14 says. All this is true whatever be the kind of business that occupies our Day, whatever be the sort of entries that fill our Diary. It is common-sense: a thing highly esteemed in James' eyes; but there is something missing—note then,

A MAN'S DUTY

"Ye ought to say, If the LORD will". Ought—duty: these are words not greatly in favour to-day. In older, sturdier times, they were amongst the unchallengeable springs of behaviour. A thing was done not because it had better be done, but because it ought to be done. I note, by the way, that, in our English New Testament, the word "ought" comes over fifty times! It is an interesting thing that, according to Matthew Henry, a very similar phrase was invariably used by the ancient Greeks, in relation to their god, in the beginning of every undertaking—the words are to be translated, "with God": that is, with—GOD'S leave, by GOD'S blessing, we will do such and such. Whether that rather sweeping "every" is justifiable or not, I do not know; but the worthy old commentator has certain support from no less an authority than the learned archæologist, the late Professor Deissmann, who, in his Light from the Ancient East, produces a photograph of a papyrus letter, in which the phrase and usage occur, and says that "the formula occurs frequently elsewhere". Our only comment just now is that, if a heathen worshipper will form the habit of thus relating the events of his life to his deity, we Christians should not be behindhand in subscribing to so admirable a custom. Certainly, we of all men "ought to say 'If the LORD will. . . .'"

Reference to GOD'S will—is the thing which was absent from the man's Diary that was set out for us in the earlier verses of our passage; but it is a man's Duty, certainly a Christian man's duty, to refer everything to that Will, to acknowledge every plan, every hope, as dependent upon that Will. The omission of this principle is not only foolishness, but it is wrong—it is a not doing of what we know full well to be right and good; and of that verse 17 says that "it is sin". Across all the pages and entries of our diary of proposed engagements must, in duty bound, be written "Deo volente", D.V., GOD willing. James is not the only one who impresses this duty upon us; for Paul also, not so much by his exhortation as by his example, teaches us the same lesson. We think of his purpose to return again to Ephesus "if GOD will", in Acts xviii. 21; and we remember his avowed intention to visit Corinth "if the LORD will", in 1 Corinthians iv. 19. So we are to fill up our Diary on the supposition that, D.V., "we shall live", as verse 15 directs us; and we are to plan our Day on the assumption that, D.V., we shall "do this, or that". All vainglorious "boastings" of our future are ruled out as "evil" (verse 16). Recall that eminently successful business man whom our LORD called a "fool", and whose folly lay in the fact that all his plannings were made without reference to GOD: his story is in Luke xii. 16*f*.

Deference to GOD'S will—is the next step to be taken. It is not treated, except implicitly, in our passage; but it so naturally follows upon what we have already said, that we should feel our study incomplete if we did not, however briefly, refer to it. It is our duty, then, not only to acknowledge that there is a Will of GOD for our lives—whether the whole of them, or the parts of them—but also to accept, and acquiesce in, that Will. How movingly we find our LORD deferring to the Father's will in Gethsemane, "Not My will, but Thine, be done", Luke xxii. 42. We have found the ultimate key to all peace when, by His grace, we have learned to make His will our will. Thus, when we say, as we ought, "If the LORD will", it is not only a reference, but a deference, to that Will. One further step remains—

Preference for GOD'S will—which means that we accept it, not only because we have to, but because we love to. Too long, and too often, we have thought of GOD'S will as something to be suffered—to be endured, instead of embraced. But all who really surrender themselves wholly to it soon "prove" for themselves, as Romans xii. 1 says, how "good and acceptable and perfect" it is. Whatever be the circumstances that enter, and control, our lives, if we are Christians they come within that limit of what "the LORD wills"—and His will for us is His best for us. We have rather got away from our business man; but these things are as true for business life—His will, either "this, or that"; whether "gain", or loss. Home life, social life, business life, spiritual life, personal life—the old hymn has it right,

"Thy wonderful grand will, my GOD
With triumph now I make it mine;
And faith shall cry a joyous Yes!
To every dear command of Thine!"

So, in all our plannings, hopings, doings, we ought to say, D.V. The plain truth is, that things will only happen D.V.; and the real joy comes when we want them only to happen D.V.

MONEY! MONEY! MONEY!

G

JAMES V. 1-6

1 Go to now, *ye* rich men, weep and howl for your miseries that shall come upon *you.*

2 Your riches are corrupted, and your garments are moth eaten.

3 Your gold and silver is cankered; and the rust of them shall be a witness against you, and shall eat your flesh as it were fire. Ye have heaped treasure together for the last days.

4 Behold, the hire of the labourers who have reaped down your fields, which is of you kept back by fraud, crieth: and the cries of them which have reaped are entered into the ears of the Lord of sabaoth.

5 Ye have lived in pleasure on the earth, and been wanton; ye have nourished your hearts, as in a day of slaughter.

6 Ye have condemned *and* killed the just; *and* he doth not resist you.

MONEY! MONEY! MONEY!

V. 1-6

WHAT a blessing! Yes—and what a curse! It all depends upon the way we look at it, and the way we use it. Perhaps our first reaction upon reading this passage is that it cannot have anything to do with believers. Some of the commentators, indeed, say that these verses are addressed to non-Christians. But, then, the Epistle as a whole, like all the Epistles, is certainly written to believers, and would be seen and read only by such; so what would be the point of including a section to unbelievers? Moreover, we have seen those who would certainly call themselves Christians who have been so spoiled by the coming of riches that the terms of this paragraph could, alas, sadly be applied to them.

Let it be said straightaway that there is nothing necessarily, nor intrinsically, wrong in being wealthy. Joseph of Arimathæa must have been considerably well-off, or he could never have taken the place and part he did in connection with our LORD's burial. Barnabas was manifestly well-to-do, and surrendered no small a sum to the common fund of the earliest band of the believers. Many people think that there are indications in the story to suggest that Martha, Mary and Lazarus were at the least comfortably placed. Certainly Abraham, "the friend of GOD", was a very affluent man. Yet in no case is there the slightest hint that these were wrong in retaining their wealth. The fact is that the harm comes not when we possess riches, but when riches possess us. That is how it was with the rich young ruler—"he had great possessions", yes; but his possessions had him. That is the reason why he was told he must give them up, while others have had no such leading.

Do you remember the grave warning addressed by Paul to young Timothy? It is in 1 Timothy vi. 9-11: "But they that *will* be rich, fall into temptation, and a snare, and into many foolish and hurtful lusts, which drown men in destruction and perdition. For *the love* of money is the root of all evil; which while some coveted after, they have erred from the faith, and pierced themselves through with many sorrows. But thou, O man of GOD, flee these things. . . ." It seems difficult to imagine that so keen a young servant of CHRIST should need such a warning. Yet, who knows? I dare say that Demas was, at one time, no less keen; but he forsook the Way, because of his love of the world—John Bunyan evidently thinks it was love of the riches of the world. You will recall him and his silver mine, which very nearly stumbled Christian in the Pilgrim's Progress. As we said earlier in this study, we have ourselves known some who lost all the fine keenness that they once had for the things of GOD because of the lure of money. Once they loved His house, and the Word, and the Prayer Meeting, and the Open Air; once they were eager to win souls, anxious above all else to please GOD. But all that is a thing of the past, their "first love" cooled, and now they care "for none of these things"—and all because of Money! Money! Money! So, let us all take warning as we consider these rather dreadful verses concerning some who gained, or used, their riches unworthily. There was—

IDLE WEALTH

Such is the teaching of verses 2 and 3. The riches of those days largely consisted of gorgeous apparel and precious metals. Think of Achan's confession in Joshua vii. 21, "I saw . . . a goodly Babylonish garment, and two hundred shekels of silver, and a wedge of gold of fifty shekels weight". Or, think of Naaman's conception of his curer's fee in 2 Kings v. 5, "Ten talents of silver, and six thousand pieces of gold, and ten changes of raiment". All this the rich men of our passage had laboriously accumulated, and studiously hoarded; and there it lay almost all of it idle, with the result that "your garments are moth eaten; your gold and silver is cankered"!

"The rust of them shall be a witness against you, and shall eat your flesh as it were fire". Rust is (*a*) *A symbol of disuse;* and this verse may properly convict us not only of unused money; but of unused gifts, which might have been so happily, and so fruitfully, employed in GOD'S service; also, of an unused Bible, whose inspired pages hold such mighty blessings, untasted because unturned; and, of an unused life, missing all the joy of His work here, and all the reward of it hereafter. Oh, how sad is "the rust of them". This is, too (*b*) *A symbol of destruction;* for nothing "eats" into the very soul like the love of money—how cankered is the very countenance of a miser! Do you remember Milton's lines describing the demon of greed—

"Mammon the least erected spirit that fell
From heaven; for even in heaven his looks and thoughts
Were always downward bent, admiring more
The riches of heaven's pavement, trodden gold,
Than aught divine or holy else enjoyed
In vision beatific!"

Here is, also—

TAINTED WEALTH

So does verse 4 make clear. "*The hire of the labourers*" —their wages were, by a merciful provision, supposed to be paid each evening as they ceased work. Look at Deuteronomy xxiv. 15 on the point, "At his day [that is, at the end of his day] thou shalt give him his hire, neither shall the sun go down upon it; for he is poor, and setteth his heart upon it". You will remember our LORD's parable where, in Matthew xx. 8, "when even was come, the lord of the vineyard saith unto his steward, Call the labourers, and give them their hire". These humble folks needed their day's wage, to carry on with. Yet, by these rich men, it was

"*Kept back by fraud*"—paltry faults were found in their work, petty excuses were made for postponement of the payment, and no doubt it often happened that the wages were overlooked entirely, for there was little redress. By such despicable frauds was the "pile" of many a well-off employer of labour increased—and the little amounts which would mean so much to the humble labourer were "kept back". I wonder if I might interject an "aside" at this point—just to enquire whether we are always as careful as we ought to be about paying those little bills, which mean so much to the small shopkeeper?

Well, "*the cries of them . . . are entered into the ears of the Lord*"—you rich men, says James, can cheat the labourers, but you can't cheat the Lord. Those cries of disappointment and distress, against which you slam your doors and shut your ears, are heard by Him. Ever since we were told in Exodus iii. 7 that He had "heard their cry", we have been assured that He always does hear the cry of the oppressed! Think again of these rich men's money; it is—

SELF-INDULGENT WEALTH

We see that in verse 5. "*Ye have lived in pleasure . . . and been wanton.*" What of their money was not hoarded, was squandered on self and sin. They saved, not for any provident motive (*a*) to put by for a rainy day, or (*b*) to make provision for the benefit of others coming after, but only that they might have a full store from which to feed their self-indulgence. As Dr. Charles Brown says, "therein lay their folly, but beneath the folly lay the sin, and it is the sin that James denounces".

Moreover, "*Ye have nourished your heart as in a day of slaughter*". The picture is that of a beast who is unconsciously fattening himself for the shambles. When that dreadful day of slaughter arrives, these who have made themselves fat, with all their shameful indulgence, will be the first to attract the attention of the slaughterer, and the first to be taken by him. Thus it fell out in course of time. Meanwhile, note this once more as—

Ruthless Wealth

This is the point of verse 6. It brushes aside everything, and every one, that stands in its way. "*Ye have condemned* and killed"—the word "condemned" suggests that these tyrants have recourse to the courts to secure their nefarious ends. Some wretched charge will be preferred, some "trumped-up" cases, against the supposed offender; a verdict will be secured; a sentence of death will be passed. To get money, money, money—they have not hesitated to take the most extreme measures.

All this barefaced robbery and murder is against "*the just*"—men who are thoroughly decent and true and upright, and whose only crime is that they stand in the way of their rapacious tormentors. What care these latter the suffering and loss they inflict upon others so long as they themselves are enriched?

And "*he doth not resist you*"—he can't, poor fellow. He is in no position to stand up to such powerful persons; and surely the very helplessness of the victims aggravates the offence. But these ill-gotten gains are—

PERISHABLE WEALTH

Let us go back to verse 1 and verse 3. "*Weep and howl for your miseries which shall come upon you*"; and "*ye have heaped treasure together for the last days*". This is the demonstrative Oriental fashion of showing distress. Matthew Henry's comment is exceedingly vivid, if not scrupulously polite: he says, "Those who live like beasts are called to howl like such". The great and overwhelming trouble which James was prophesying seems to be the impending judgment upon the Holy City, a catastrophe which affected, not only those who, at the time, were actually resident in Jerusalem, but also those Jews who had become scattered abroad—for whom, as we have seen, this Epistle was particularly written. It is to be noted that the wealthier Jews everywhere lost everything. They had, indeed, "heaped treasure together", but what did it profit them, what did they gain for all their pains? Truly, it only awaited "the last days" of that age, which were fast running out when James was writing, for it all to be completely lost. What a pity, then, that they had given their undivided attention to the accumulation of material riches, and had devoted no thought at all to becoming "rich in faith", as James ii. 5 has it, "rich toward GOD", as Luke xii. 21 would instruct us. What a pity, I say, that amongst all their "heaped treasure", there was no "treasure in heaven", where, as the Master said, in Matthew vi. 20, "neither moth nor rust doth corrupt, and where thieves do not break through nor steal". All this latter is imperishable wealth, and its acquisition abundantly justifies all our strivings, all our prayers, all our sacrifices. To heap this up "for the last days" is to provide for our great comfort, for our richest joy, for our eternal blessedness, and for our Master's glory.

. . . . .

Still, it is of material riches that James is led by the HOLY SPIRIT to write; and his words are a stern and solemn warning to us all to give good heed to the manner in which we use the Money—whether much, or little—that we have. One thinks almost instinctively of those words with which the Master makes application of His parable of the unjust steward, in Luke xvi. 9: "Make to yourselves friends of the mammon of unrighteousness; that, when ye fail, they may receive you into everlasting habitations." It seems, as it stands, a somewhat cryptic utterance; but a little careful consideration of its terms will perhaps make its meaning clearer. It is well to get a real understanding of it, even if only for the fact that its implications do give us a very useful finishing point for our study on the use of money.

Let us, then, first of all, look at some of the words and phrases in the verse—(i) "of", means "by means of". (ii) "the mammon of unrighteousness" is a term for Money, called so because of the mischief it is capable of doing in the realms of Sin and Self, and because, to quote again Paul's word to Timothy, "the love of money is the root of all kinds of evil", 1 Timothy vi. 10, R.V. (iii) "when ye fail", means, I think, simply, when you die. (iv) "receive you", is only another way of saying "welcome you". (v) "everlasting habitations", refers to the eternal dwelling-place on the other side. So much for the actual words employed.

Having now arrived at the probable significance of our terms, we are in a position to get the drift of the whole passage. In the light of what we have said, perhaps a paraphrase will be the most helpful thing at this point. This is how Dr. Moffatt has it: "Use mammon [money] . . . to make friends for yourselves, so that when you die they may welcome you to the eternal abodes".

Here is somebody who out of his substance (small or great) contributes, in some way, to the spread of the preaching of the Gospel. Through that agency, the Gospel reaches the ears, heart, and life of an unbeliever, who is consequently saved by His grace, and subsequently ushered into His everlasting habitation. What a welcome that redeemed soul will have ready in Heaven for that (at present) unknown Somebody who by his money made possible that preaching of the Gospel that reached him. In the words of the old hymn, "Was that Somebody you?" How well worth while it is to use your substance for such furthering of the ministry of the Gospel, whether through individuals, or through churches, or through societies; and what eternal friends you will thus make for yourself by means of your money!

Next in importance only to this primary duty of the believer, comes that other happy burden laid upon us to use so much of our means (whether plenty or scanty) as we can for helping on GOD'S poor—seeking to be wise, and discriminating, and sympathetic, and understanding, in our help. So are we urged—both by the teaching of our LORD, and by the passage of James, not to hoard our money, not to spend it on the indulgence of self, but, in a phrase of Dr. Torrey's, to "invest it in heavenly and abiding securities". Not least amongst the returns that such investments will bring us will be the glad and grateful welcome we shall get up yonder from the poor that we have helped to succour, and from the sinners that we have helped to save.

Yes, Money! Money! Money!—after all, what a blessing it can be.

IF THE OUTLOOK BE DARK, TRY THE UPLOOK

JAMES V. 7-12

7 Be patient therefore, brethren, unto the coming of the Lord. Behold, the husbandman waiteth for the precious fruit of the earth, and hath long patience for it, until he receive the early and latter rain.

8 Be ye also patient; stablish your hearts: for the coming of the Lord draweth nigh.

9 Grudge not one against another, brethren, lest ye be condemned: behold, the judge standeth before the door.

10 Take, my brethren, the prophets, who have spoken in the name of the Lord, for an example of suffering affliction, and of patience.

11 Behold, we count them happy which endure. Ye have heard of the patience of Job, and have seen the end of the Lord; that the Lord is very pitiful, and of tender mercy.

12 But above all things, my brethren, swear not, neither by heaven, neither by the earth, neither by any other oath: but let your yea be yea, and *your* nay, nay; lest ye fall into condemnation.

IF THE OUTLOOK BE DARK, TRY THE UPLOOK

V. 7-12

SIX times over in this brief passage the thought of patience (or, long-suffering) and endurance is found. The fact is, that these early believers had to live their Christian life in the midst of most difficult circumstances; they were beset with problems, and persecutions. I sometimes wonder whether we should stand firm and keen if it meant that we must suffer for our faith: what a little ridicule it takes to send us into our shells! For those to whom James writes, the outlook is very dark, so he invites them to try the uplook. He encourages them with the thought that "the coming of the LORD draweth nigh", v. 7, 8. George Meredith has somewhere a lovely phrase, concerning "the rapture of the forward view". Those of you who have had to spend a long period away from home, and then find yourselves able to undertake a visit to the old folks and fireside, know something about this "rapture". Why, even an old horse knows it, when nearing home after a long day's grind. Meredith did not, I fear, have the Second Advent in mind when he wrote the words; but we may so appropriately borrow and apply them to our theme—which Titus ii. 13 refers to as "that blessed hope": "happy" hope, if you like, for so much hangs upon His Coming to make it a joyous thing.

It will usher in for us (*a*) *Unbroken Friendship*—this present life is marked and marred by separations; but then, as the great New Testament commentator, Henry Alford, wrote, in his famous hymn, "What knitting severed friendships up, where partings are no more". (*b*) *Unhindered*

Service—love longs to serve Him, but here is so hindered, by shyness, and weakness, and poverty, and nerves, and ignorance, and self, and fatigue, and fear; but there "His servants shall serve Him" without let or hindrance. (*c*) *Unclouded Vision*—a real sight of Him, which the restrictions and inhibitions of our human nature made impossible down here. (*d*) *Unsullied Likeness*—instead of that pale and spotted imitation of His image that is all some of us have shewn on earth, "we shall be like Him" perfectly; which is one of the mightiest miracles of the Second Advent. (*e*) *Unravelled skeins*—all our tangled and torturing problems solved and straightened out. All this, and much more besides, is wrapped up in His return—a "happy hope", indeed; a rapturous "forward view"; an up-look which will shed some heartening light into the darkest out-look! Let us now see how the matter is treated in our passage; and note how the Saviour is apparently pictured as returning in a threefold capacity.

The Husbandman Reaping His Harvest

"Behold the Husbandman," says v. 7. This may be just an illustration used for the purpose of kindling our patience to "wait" for the after-results of all our toil and suffering. On the other hand, it may well be employed as a picture of the Lord Himself, using all the means at His divine disposal to bring about a harvest of character in our lives—a picture which shews Him to be waiting with such "long patience", and which encourages us to "be . . . also patient", knowing that He has the matter in hand. The first thing to remember, though it is not dealt with in our passage, is (i) *The expenditure on the field.* The identity of that field is not far to seek, for, as 1 Corinthians iii. 9 tells us, "*ye* are God's husbandry". The purchase price was Precious Blood, for "ye were not redeemed with corruptible things as ['little bits of' Greek] silver and gold . . .

but with the precious blood of CHRIST", 1 Peter i. 18-9. Further expenditure upon the field consists of the exercise of all the love and power of GOD for its fruitfulness. Indeed, to quote His enquiry made in another connection, in Isaiah v. 4, "What could have been done more . . . that I have not done in it?"

Think then of (ii) *The experience of the field.* How dependent it is upon the weather—even the varieties of weather. The passage speaks of the "rain". In Palestine there are but two seasons—a wet, from October to April; and a dry, from May to September, during which there will normally be not one drop of rain. The former period is obviously of tremendous importance to the field and to the Husbandman. The harvest depends, first, upon the "early rain", which generally falls from October to December. If it delay, they must with "long patience" wait for it; because, during the long dry season, the ground has become as hard as iron, and without the early rain there can be no ploughing, no sowing. Then, at the close of the wet season, comes the "latter rain", in March and April, without which there will be no harvest. The rain may not always be pleasant, but it is essential to harvest. Other kinds of weather, too, are necessary. The sun, of course; though, as a Spanish proverb has it, "All sunshine makes a desert"—it is not good for us that our lives should be "all sunshine", in spite of Faber's hymn; the frost—which will kill off a good many enemies of the crops; the lightning—which, besides cleaning the air, will manufacture nitrogen compounds from the air, and spread them over the ground; the snow—a lovely warm blanket, with its electrical properties, for the seedlings below ground; the wind—vigorously and healthily shaking the growth above ground. But, principally, the rain. Much of all this is typical of the soul's weather, the often hard and bitter experience of the field. We must with patience wait and, if needs be, suffer, that the fruit may appear in due time. That great American preacher, Henry Ward Beecher, has a delightful passage on this need of patience: he says, "O impatient ones! Did the leaves say nothing to you as they murmured when you came hither to-day? They were not created this spring, but months ago; and the summer, just begun, will fashion others for another year. At the bottom of every leaf-stem is a cradle, and in it is an infant germ; and the winds will rock it, and the birds will sing to it all summer long; and next season it will unfold. So GOD is working for you, and carrying forward to the perfect development all the processes of your lives". Yes, that's it; GOD at work, the Husbandman at work, in all the experiences, sad or glad, of the succeeding days.

And thus we come to (iii) *The expectation from the field.* Verse 7 describes it as "the precious fruit of the earth". The "precious seed" of which Psalm cxxvi. 6 speaks has thus been brought to its fruition. Bought with "precious blood", sown with "precious seed", laden with "precious fruit"—that is the holy sequence which awakens the expectation of the returning Husbandman as He comes to reap His harvest. Will He be, in us, disappointed of His expectation? Will the harvest be green, instead of golden? Well, it largely depends on the patient endurance of the troublous experiences of life. If that be right, we may joyously await His coming and find help in the Uplook as comfort for the Outlook; and, for His part, as Isaiah liii. 11 promised Him, "He shall see of the travail of His soul, and shall be satisfied". Profound and overwhelming mystery as it is, He shall count all His expenditure on the field as having been worth while. Let this thought "stablish your hearts", as verse 8 says; let it steady you to face whatever weather shall come to your soul. And so our passage leads us to another aspect of the Master's return—

THE JUDGE ANNOUNCING HIS DECISION

"The Judge standeth before the door", according to v. 9—"the doors", as the original has it. There is no doubt that the "glorious appearing" of our Lord JESUS CHRIST is a most happy event; but let us never forget that it is also a matter of great seriousness and solemnity, for connected with it is the Judgment of Believers, of which Paul is led to write, in Romans xiv. 10, that "we shall all stand before the judgment-seat of CHRIST", and which he elaborates with considerable detail in 1 Corinthians iii. 9*c*-15, warning us that "the fire shall try every man's work of what sort [not, 'size'] it is". Because that lies ahead, we are here urged to be careful concerning our behaviour towards our fellow-believers, in regard to this matter of hard experience in the world outside. It is, as we all know, so possible to stand undefeated and undaunted in the conflict with the world, and yet, by reason of the strain and stress upon our very nerves occasioned by the struggle, to fail amongst ourselves. Missionaries in a foreign land have sometimes had evidence of the insidiousness of this danger in the domestic relationships with their fellow-missionaries. Indeed, we all know it; and James seems here, in his own practical fashion, to turn aside, in verses 9 and 10, to warn these early Christians about it, discussing the matter in the light of the Master's sure return to judge them for their after-conversion life and conduct and service.

He calls attention to the fact that (*a*) *Their lives were in danger of getting distraught.* "One against another, brethren"—is the trouble; so fierce is the fight outside, that it is liable to take physical toll of them, and to produce, inside, jangled nerves and frayed tempers. Thanks to the indwelling SPIRIT of GOD it need not be so; but if He be not in control it can so easily become so. And what is it all about? "Grudge not"—more exactly, "groan not"! Have you ever come across groaning Christians—those who are always grousing and grumbling, muttering and moaning? Matthew Henry has his own way of summing them up: "Murmuring groans at what befalls you; distrustful groans as to what may further come; revengeful groans against the instruments of your sufferings; envious groans at those who have not such calamities". What havoc to happy Christian fellowship is wrought by all this.

Note further that (b) *Their language was a mirror of their minds' disturbance.* Uncertain of themselves, they had become accustomed to embellish their utterance with oaths invoking the aid, or testimony, of "heaven" or "earth", in explosive and vehement speech, when, as verse 12 tells them, they should "swear not", but be satisfied that their plain straightforward statements—be they "Yea", "Nay", or anything else—should suffice. But, you see, this excited, unguarded, manner of talk was all symptomatic, and would come under the "condemnation" of the coming Lord. How often, and how solemnly, has James warned us, throughout the Epistle, about our tongues!

That all this need not be is plainly indicated by the fact that (c) *Their lessons were set unmistakably before them.* "The prophets", whose teaching they were so familiar with, were splendid lessons for them—each an "example" of the way "affliction" should be borne. They spoke, with all the authority of Divine leading, not their own thoughts and views and opinions, but GOD'S mind—their messages were "spoken in the Name of the Lord" But the point here is that practice corresponded with precept, life coincided with lip. They exhorted to patience, and themselves exhibited it. Like Bishop Armstrong's teachers—

> "Themselves first training for the skies,
> They best will raise their people there."

"Take", for instance, Jeremiah and Hosea, what "suffering affliction" was theirs; yet did they not murmur nor complain, but bore it all with exemplary "patience". James would have his readers follow their example; and the HOLY SPIRIT, through him, would have us also fall into line.

For, they were reminded that (*d*) *Their Lord was assuredly coming to judge them.* Don't groan at your lot, don't grouse at your fellow Christian—you will assuredly be "condemned" for such things; and, in any case, how infinitely wiser and happier it is to leave things in His hands, and to await His decision upon things and people. "The judge standeth at the door"—how vivid a description of the imminence of His appearing: we picture an earthly judge, standing on the inner side of those doors, awaiting only the striking of the hour, about to come into court. How vivid is the picture! We recall that other phrase, in Genesis iv. 7, "If thou doest not well, sin lieth at the door"—that is, a sin-offering lieth at the door. A sacrificial victim was near at hand for Cain's use, as GOD had evidently planned. Our Lord JESUS, as the Sin-Bearer, is at the very door of every sinner's easy reach; and, as the Judge, He is standing "at the door", awaiting the striking of the hour. Let us put to ourselves the solemn enquiry—what decision will He announce respecting our own selves and the way we have followed Him, even in our distresses? Will it be "Well done"? Well, now let us go on to one further aspect of His return—

THE LORD DISCLOSING HIS PURPOSE

"Ye have seen the end of the Lord," says v. 11. He always works toward some "end"; in His children's lives, and through their varied, and sometimes painful, circumstances, He is always working for their "good", as Romans viii. 28 expresses it, always pursuing some blessed purpose for them; and when He comes, He will disclose it to our astonished eyes—some day we'll understand, and praise His Name.

James has been speaking of the patience of the prophets, and so naturally old Job comes to his mind—"ye have heard of his patience". (*a*) *His experience*—how terribly hard it all seemed; yet with what patience he met it all. (*b*) *His ignorance*—he simply couldn't understand why it was allowed. He knew that "the LORD is very pitiful and of tender mercy", although it didn't look like it; but he went on trusting. (*c*) *His recompense*—came at last, came in this life. Two words of Job xlii. 12 express it, "more than". He had had so much, he had lost so much; but GOD'S "end" for him even here was "more than"! For ourselves, one of the joys of "the other side", after He has come for us, will be to see what His purpose for us was, and how wonderfully He worked it out.

After a shocking pit disaster, the late Bishop of Durham, the saintly Handley Moule, went to try to comfort the stricken villagers, gathered in their grief at the pithead. He held up before them a treasured book-marker—all they saw, for he turned to them its wrong side, was a meaningless, seemingly purposeless, tangle of threads—what meaning could these dark and bitter experiences have? Then he shewed them the other side; and they saw the words (and the truth) "GOD is love". He is coming to shew us the other side; so, if the outlook be dark, try the uplook!

CAMEL-KNEES

JAMES I. 5-8: IV. 2-3; V. 13-20

5 If any of you lack wisdom, let him ask of God, that giveth to all *men* liberally, and upbraideth not; and it shall be given him.

6 But let him ask in faith, nothing wavering. For he that wavereth is like a wave of the sea driven with the wind and tossed.

7 For let not that man think that he shall receive any thing of the Lord.

8 A double minded man *is* unstable in all his ways.

. . . . .

ye fight and war, yet ye have not, because ye ask not.

3 Ye ask, and receive not, because ye ask amiss, that ye may consume *it* upon your lusts.

. . . . .

13 Is any among you afflicted? let him pray. Is any merry? let him sing psalms.

14 Is any sick among you? let him call for the elders of the church; and let them pray over him, anointing him with oil in the name of the Lord:

15 And the prayer of faith shall save the sick, and the Lord shall raise him up; and if he have committed sins, they shall be forgiven him.

16 Confess *your* faults one to another, and pray one for another, that ye may be healed. The effectual fervent prayer of a righteous man availeth much.

17 Elias was a man subject to like passions as we are, and he prayed earnestly that it might not rain; and it rained not on the earth by the space of three years and six months.

18 And he prayed again, and the heaven gave rain, and the earth brought forth her fruit.

19 Brethren, if any of you do err from the truth, and one convert him,

20 Let him know, that he which converteth the sinner from the error of his way shall save a soul from death, and shall hide a multitude of sins.

CAMEL-KNEES

I. 5-8; IV. 2-3; V. 13-20

YOU may wonder at the somewhat strange title that heads this study. It was the nickname that the early church gave to the writer of this Epistle. It is said that his knees were as hard as camel's knees; and the reason for that is not far to seek—he was a great man of prayer, and was so constantly on his knees that they had worn hard! As he was himself so earnest a practitioner in prayer, he has every right to expect us to listen to him, when he writes on the subject, as he does so frequently in his brief Letter. The two matters that James deals with most often are—Tongues, and Knees. It is the latter that is to occupy our attention now; and, as we have read through the chosen passage, I dare say that one of the chief impressions made on your mind was, that it seems that there is no legitimate aspect of human life in which prayer may not play an important, indeed a decisive, part. For example—

MENTAL THINGS

The Christian life has its difficulties in the realm of the mind; and in these verses of chapter i., James takes up one such: (*a*) *The need for wisdom*—the context is dealing with the trials and tribulations which vex and test the lives of us all, seeing that "we are all in the same boat". Why all this is allowed was a perplexing problem in those days, even as in ours; and a wisdom more than human was needed to tackle the matter. That is only one amongst the myriad difficulties, doubts and distresses that harass the Christian from time to time. A thousand situations arise in which we become acutely conscious that we "lack wisdom". So we turn, here, with alacrity, to (*b*) *The fount of wisdom*—"GOD", who is not only All-loving, and All-powerful, but All-wise as well; and who "giveth", not keeping the boon of His wisdom from those who need it so much; who, moreover, deals so "liberally" in this matter, being never niggardly in His giving; and how good it is to remember that He "upbraideth not". We so often spoil our gifts by first upbraiding the necessitous recipients, but GOD never deals with us in that fashion. He does not tell us that we come too often, nor that we ask too much. Well; and what is (*c*) *The channel of wisdom?* "Let him ask"—prayer has its part to play; but "let him ask in faith". If we are quite sure in our own mind that, in any matter, we really do want only GOD'S will and GOD'S glory, then we may "ask in faith", being confident that, in His own way, we shall be given wisdom and guidance; we may not recognise it at the time, but, on looking back, we shall see how true it is that, as Psalm xxxvii. 23 says, "the steps of a good man are ordered by the LORD". Prayer has its place, too, in—

NATIONAL THINGS

When we were dealing with iv. 2-3 the other day, we saw that the fightings and wars referred to were probably the personal squabbles, bickerings, animosities, and antagonisms that so often disfigure Christian lives. Yet we may say, without straining, that if the words refer to them, they may also apply to all kinds of war-like relationships, whether as between individuals, or nations. I make no apology, then, for introducing the national condition into this paragraph. It is to be noted that we have here three "nots"—three missing things: (*a*) *The missing victory*—"ye fight and war, yet ye have not": you have so much, perhaps—a magnificent force, a righteous cause, an inflexible will, a glorious courage; but with all this, victory delays. Why? (*b*) *The missing weapon*—"because ye ask not": we say that we want more guns, more planes, more shells, more tanks, more men, more money, and too often we forget that, above all else, we need more prayers! If we would use our knees more, it would be well indeed. There is an animal in South Africa, called the gnu, which has a curious method of meeting its enemies. Whenever it is going to attack, it first gets down on its knees, and gets its impetus from that attitude, it springs best from the kneeling position! What a sensible beast; and what an example for us all. But see the third "not" in this passage, (*c*) *The missing technique*—"ye ask and receive not, because ye ask amiss". We may pray, and yet fail, because we pray wrongly; there are conditions, rules, a spiritual technique. The one point mentioned in the passage is, Motive: if you only seek the blessing—in this case, the victory—"that ye may consume it upon your lusts", that is, to satisfy your own desires and wishes, to further your own ends, you need not be surprised if you fail of your prayer. Next, prayer may effect—

Emotional Things

That seems to me to be a reasonable inference from the words of verse 13 of our 5th chapter. We have the two extremes of emotion here—down in the depths, up on the heights; "afflicted . . . merry". What are we to do with our great emotional experiences? This verse teaches us to relate them to God. (*a*) *In the one case*—"let him pray". Whatever else he does in his distress, let him do that. Maybe, his trouble will be so devastating that he will feel he cannot pray—well, at least, if he cannot frame a petition, let him simply tell God his trouble, like those bereft souls in Matthew xiv. 12, who just "went and told Jesus". The old hymn says—

"Oh, what peace we often forfeit,
Oh, what needless pain we bear,
All because we do not carry
Everything to God in prayer."

Just to tell Him, brings such ease, and such peace. (*b*) *In the other case*—"let him sing". The word translated "merry" means "well in mind", which only shows what God thinks of gladness, and of gloom. Now this emotion also is to be related to Him; so "let him sing". But he must choose his song aright. Certainly, he can't go wrong if he choose "psalms". What a lot there is in the Bible—in both Old and New Testaments—about songs and singing. Don't forget that praise is a part of prayer. Then come—

Physical Things

Verses 14 and 15 are, in some ways, rather difficult; but they are full of interest. Let us see first of all (*a*) *What is not taught here*. To begin with (i) That sickness is the result of sin. That was an idea widely held even in our Lord's day, as John ix. 2 indicates; and, at the present day, there are those who hold that so much is this the case that sickness needs to be dealt with by the Atonement, and that, on that ground, all illness can, and should, be healed. Note, however, that "if", at the end of verse 15: the former part of the statement has no suggestion of any connection between suffering and sin; but, of course, there are some cases in which iniquity is the root cause of the trouble, as in the example of the Man sick of the Palsy, whose Wickedness was dealt with before his Weakness, Mark ii. 5, 11. Well, says our passage, "if" that be so, he shall have forgiveness, as well as healing; but the two evils are not necessarily connected. (ii) That Extreme Unction is commanded. We are all aware of the practice of the Roman Church, based on this very verse.

When a sick man is "in extremis", he is anointed with oil, to help him over Death; but this passage has no possible relation to such a custom, for the oil is here intended to help him back to life! (iii) That the use of means for healing is wrong. Such is not the teaching of this Scripture. Indeed, there are not a few commentators who incline to the view that the very "oil" mentioned here is medicinal, inasmuch as the most widely-used remedies of the time were "oil and wine", Luke x. 34. But, of course, the fact is that the point here is not, Means or no means, but Prayer or no prayer. If means are wrong, it seems strange that the always "out and out" Paul was so friendly with Luke "the beloved Physician", as he calls him, in Colossians iv. 14, and whom there is reason to believe he first met when he called him in as his medical attendant at Troas; strange, also, is it that he recommended means to his young and delicate friend Timothy, when, in 1 Timothy v. 23, he advised him to "use a little wine for thy stomach's sake and thine often infirmities". I often wonder why those who advocate what they call Divine Healing, without means, are themselves so inconsistent as to wear spectacles, and have false-teeth? However, the matter is settled for me by the words of our LORD, when He said, in Matthew ix. 12, that sick people needed doctors: "They that be whole need not a physician, but they that are sick".

It is full time that we considered (*b*) *What is taught here*. (i) That we may pray—"let them pray over him". In a hundred passages, besides this one, we are encouraged to bring our sick ones to the Throne of Grace, and to make our bodily needs a matter of prayer. Our Father-hearted (Psalm ciii. 13), Mother-hearted (Isaiah lxvi. 13), Brother-hearted (Hebrews ii. 11), GOD is tenderly sympathetic towards all our ills, and would have us speak to Him about them. (ii) That it is the patient's responsibility to make his condition known—"let him send". There is no promise that the "elders" shall have mysterious powers of discovering that any member of the flock is ill, when nobody, not even the sick-one, tells them. (iii) That "the prayer of faith shall save the sick". I do not think that this refers to ordinary prayers, however good and earnest. These latter do not always ensure recovery; else, why should Paul leave poor Trophimus sick in 2 Timothy iv. 20? Do you suppose he didn't pray for him? And why should his own prayer, thrice offered, 2 Corinthians xii. 7-9, for his personal relief of bodily affliction, be denied him? The teaching here is, that the particular kind of intercession designated always "shall" ensure recovery! It is my own belief that this "prayer of faith" is not something that can be prayed at will, but that it is given of God in certain cases, to serve His own loving purposes, and in strict accordance with His sovereign will. Not all Christians are to be healed; else, how should we ever die? We must die somehow, seeing we are in this body; for the Scripture teaches us that, until Christ return, "it is appointed unto man . . . to die", Hebrews ix. 27. So then, of "any sick among you", some will succumb, and some will recover; they are all to be prayed for, but, in some cases, God will beget in the "elders" the prayer of faith. In these latter instances, the elders will have no doubt of the issue; a confidence of victory will be born in them of the Holy Spirit, even as they pray. The healing will normally come through means; sometimes, but only within His sovereign will, it will be accomplished without the use of any means whatever. In both cases, it is Divine Healing, for, which ever way it is, "the Lord shall raise him up," as v. 15 says. And now let us turn to—

Personal Things

"One for another," says verse 16. So different from the "one against another", of verse 9. (*a*) *Prayer is always the best thing*—certainly we could never do anything better for one another than to pray. Intercession for people can be such a help to them; and mind you have some on your list whom you don't like. If you pray for such long enough, and earnestly enough, you will come to see their good points, and to improve their bad ones. (*b*) *Prayer is sometimes the hard thing*—easy, perhaps, if you are friends, but what if you are at loggerheads? Oh well, in that case, you must "confess your faults one to another". It is "faults", not "sins"; the former word is, according to some of the old texts, a quite different one in the Greek from the usual word for "sins", found in the previous verse. This is no incitement to secret confession of sins to a priest, nor open confession of sins as with the Oxford Groups; this is mutual confession of faults to those whom we have wronged. "That ye may be healed", may very well refer to spiritual recovery, rather than physical, for the word is quite often used in that sense: for example, "Lest . . . they . . . should be converted, and I should heal them", Matthew xiii. 15, and "let it rather be healed", Hebrews xii. 13; and "by whose stripes ye were healed", 1 Peter ii. 24. How many quarrels and estrangements would be thus healed, if only we followed this inspired teaching about mutual confession of "fault" and earnest prayer "one for another". (*c*) *Prayer is certainly the effective thing*—as that closing bit of our verse makes plain; but (i) the man, must be "righteous", holy in life and (ii) the manner, must be "fervent", his whole heart being in it, and then (iii) the "much" will be given—all of which is illustrated in the case of Elijah who is brought before us in the next verse, which suggests another legitimate sphere of prayer—

Material Things

It was about the weather that Elijah prayed; and God will certainly allow us to speak to Him about this that forms (so large a part of our conversation) so important a part of our daily lives. We are encouraged to bring all our material affairs to Him—always, of course, remembering that His will must be paramount. Elijah's was (a) *Persistent praying*—1 Kings xviii tells us the thrilling story of it, the Story of an Answer. There are three stages indicated (i) "There is nothing", v. 43; six times over there seemed to be failure, but the prophet went on, refusing to get discouraged, until (ii) "There ariseth a little cloud", v. 44; GOD'S encouragement, GOD'S earnest, GOD'S indication. Let us not however be content with "a little" blessing when GOD'S purpose is "a great" blessing. So (iii) "There was a great rain", v. 45—"great" is ever the scale of GOD'S giving, if our faith persists in prayer. It was (*b*) *Human praying*—we are not to suppose that the prophet was a being apart; he was very much one of ourselves; the passage, lest we think all this too high for ourselves, reminds us that he was "a man subject to like passions as we are", which implies that we need not despair of a successful prayer life. But this was (*c*) *Real praying*—there was nothing perfunctory, or merely formal, about it. You will notice that the marginal rendering of "he prayed earnestly" is "he prayed in prayer". How suggestive that is! Some people do anything but pray in their prayers—they use mere words, or they appear just to be giving GOD information, or they seem to be flattering the leader of the meeting, or they give the impression that they are simply performing a duty. You will recognise all these; perhaps, like the writer, you have oft-times been guilty of such supposed praying yourself. Elijah really prayed when he prayed. Then at last we come to—

SPIRITUAL THINGS

Of course, prayer has an enormous influence in this realm. (*a*) *The case in mind*—is one of eternal significance,